Praise for *Klout* M

"If you want real clout, this is the book to read."
—Randy Gage, *New York Times* bestselling author of *Risky Is the New Safe*

"You will never be a big deal online until you understand Klout. And you won't really understand Klout until you read this book. I didn't get it before. I do now."
—Larry Winget, *New York Times* bestselling author of *Grow a Pair*

"We now live in an age of influence marketing, and in order for your business to really thrive, it's critical to be strategically active on all the major social sites. In *Klout Matters*, Gina and Terry walk you through the exact steps needed to build a sizable platform, leverage key relationships, and create real influence for greater success. This book is a must-read for anyone striving to become a respected thought leader."
—Mari Smith, *Forbes* Top Ten Social Media Power Influencer 2011–2013, speaker, and author of *The New Relationship Marketing* and *Facebook Marketing*

"I'm one of the biggest Klout skeptics out there, but Carr and Brock have given me some thoughts in this book that might have me at least take a second look. This isn't to be overlooked."
—Chris Brogan, CEO and president of Human Business Works and *New York Times* bestselling author of *Trust Agents*

"*Klout Matters* is a must-read for leaders in any field who want to strategically increase their social media influence to elevate their digital brand, accelerate positive results, and stay ahead of the competition. Buy it and read it today, before your competition does!"
—Daniel Burrus, *New York Times* bestselling author of *Flash Foresight*

"A complete primer that is critically needed and will greatly benefit businesspeople, entrepreneurs, thought leaders, and anyone else who wants to have greater influence in the world of social media. Terry and Gina demystify Klout and provide usable strategies for increasing your Klout score and, more important, your impact and success. I'm glad I read it and recommend you read it too."
—Mark Sanborn, *New York Times* bestselling author of *The Fred Factor*

"This powerful, practical book shows you how to supercharge your sales with some of the most effective marketing techniques ever discovered."
—Brian Tracy, *New York Times* bestselling author of *Now . . . Build a Great Business*

"Terry and Gina give you philosophical and practical strategies for using Klout to its fullest. If you follow their advice, you will see your Klout score increase!"
—Joel Comm, *New York Times* bestselling author of *Twitter Power*

"Do you have social influence, relevance, recognition, pertinence, and significance? In other words, do you have Klout? If you want it, then social media experts Gina Carr and Terry Brock will teach you how to get it."
—Shep Hyken, *New York Times* bestselling author of *The Amazement Revolution*

"An absolute must-read if you are serious about being credible and relevant in an overly saturated marketplace. *Klout Matters* will help you outmaneuver your competition and gain serious social media altitude."
—Lt. Col. Rob "Waldo" Waldman, US Air Force (ret.), author of the *New York Times* and *Wall Street Journal* bestseller *Never Fly Solo*

"In this terrific and informative book, we learn from two of today's most savvy social-media authorities that—when it comes right down to it—it's still about the relationship. They do a magnificent job of teaching us how to utilize various social media to match high-tech with high-touch and how to tap into the power of Klout while doing it."
—Bob Burg, coauthor of *The Go-Giver* and author of *Adversaries into Allies*

"Terry Brock and Gina Carr show specific ways to leverage your Klout score to position yourself as a respected thought leader and topic expert so you dramatically increase your visibility and profitability. Read it and reap."
—Sam Horn, author of *POP!*

"The premier resource for understanding Klout and the power of online influence in today's digital world—and how to get it and use it to your advantage. A definite must-read, this is a book you will find yourself returning to often and one that you will recommend to others."
—Kim Garst, social media strategist and *Forbes* Top Twenty Social Media Women Power Influencer

"If influence is today's social currency, then this book will help you get rich. *Klout Matters* provides businesses and individuals with a road map for using Klout to leverage their influence and build vibrant online communities that will amplify their message."
　　　　—Mark Fidelman, managing director of Evolve! and author of *Socialized!*

"Reading Brock and Carr's fascinating book is an essential step in your business education. *Klout Matters* is about smart, savvy ways to increase your impact, influence, and income."
　　　　—David Newman, author of Amazon #1 bestseller *Do It! Marketing*

"Carr and Brock pull back the curtain and make your Klout score as easy to understand as your FICO and BMI scores. Executives, entrepreneurs, speakers, authors, marketers, and other thought leaders who want to connect with customers will be fascinated with this newest objective tool to measure influence."
　　　　—Dianna Booher, author of *Creating Personal Presence* and *Communicate with Confidence!*

"Terry Brock and Gina Carr give easy-to-understand examples of how not only to raise your Klout Score but also to increase business by better connecting with customers."
　　　　—Gene Griessman, PhD, author of *Time Tactics of Very Successful People*

"Anyone serious about business in today's market needs to measure their social media effectiveness. This book shows you how."
　　　　—Mary C. Kelly, PhD, Commander, U.S. Navy (ret.), and author of *15 Ways to Grow Your Business in Every Economy*

"*Klout Matters* can help you not only to raise your Klout score but also to assist you in getting more business as a thought leader. If you want that edge, buy this book and apply the very straightforward steps."
　　　　—John B. Molidor, PhD, CEO and president of Michigan State University-Flint, Area Medical Education, assistant dean and professor at Michigan State University, and author of *Crazy Good Interviewing*

"Gina Carr and Terry Brock give practical tips and tricks to managing your Klout score. Absolutely essential reading for anyone doing business online!"
　　　　—Andrea Vahl, social media and Facebook marketing expert and coauthor of *Facebook Marketing All-in-One for Dummies*

"Terry Brock and Gina Carr have penned the only book you need to read to understand and benefit from your Klout score. Read it before your competition does!"
—Corey Perlman, digital marketing speaker and author of *eBoot Camp*

"Gina Carr and Terry Brock, two very savvy marketing experts, break down what Klout means, how you can build your score, and why it should be important to you."
—Mary Jo Martin, editorial director of *The Wholesaler* magazine

"My fear of being absorbed by the Borg of social media has been replaced by the excitement of knowing what small steps I can take to begin to engage my customers in ways I am likely to enjoy—and in which they will see more of the value I can offer.
—David Gouthro, CSP, The Consulting Edge

"After applying what I learned from this book, my Klout score went up 10 points! The great thing about that is the recognition and greater business that has resulted. You guys rock!"
—J.B. Glossinger, host of *Morning Coach*, the #1 podcast on personal development

"An essential tool for raising not only your personal online impact but that of your organization, this book contains everything you need to ensure your online Klout is working for your personal brand and your corporate message."
—Lesley Everett, personal brand expert, president of Global Speakers Federation (2013-2014), and author of *Walking TALL*

"WOW! A fantastic read! Every business owner needs to listen to the advice here and carve out time to build influence."
—Gina Schreck, president and CEO of SocialKNX

"*Klout Matters* is a great tool. In addition to providing clarity about Klout with respect to all aspects of communications, Terry and Gina spell out the specifics on how to raise your digital presence."
—Bryan C. Shirley, principal at OneAccord

"Terry and Gina have written the social media bible on how to achieve and measure your results. Readers will acquire a wealth of ideas for increasing their value to their target markets and be warned about the dangers of short-term gaming tactics. Whether one is a beginner or a guru, this book will be extremely informative."
—Ken Futch, CSP, author of *Take Your Best Shot*

"Yes, it's about raising your Klout Score—a good thing—but it's really about how to be a better social media citizen, engaging more effectively with customers, and doing more and better business—which is a great thing!"

—Warren Evans, CSP, and member of the
Professional Speaking Hall of Fame (Canada)

"A crucial work. After just one week of using Terry and Gina's suggestions, my Klout score jumped 7 points."

—Ed Rigsbee, author of *The Art of Partnering*,
Developing Strategic Alliances, and *PartnerShift*

"One of the most exciting upsides of social media is that merit matters more than money, and merit is often measured by the value of our ideas. Klout Matters shows us exactly how we measure up to others, so we can get even better at what we offer, burnishing our brand, and benefitting from it."

—Kare Anderson, CEO of Say it Better Center and contributor
to *Forbes* and *Huffington Post*

"Terry and Gina cut through the noise and identify the what, why, and how of Klout. Valuable."

—Donna Hanson, technology commentator at
Prime Solutions Training & Consulting

"*Klout Matters* cuts through the trial and error that had us spending thousands on what didn't work and gives us a guide to attaining measurable, achievable results. Finally, a roadmap to influence."

—Niki Nicastro McCuistion, CSP, executive producer of
the McCuistion program on PBS

"Gina Carr and Terry Brock thoroughly examine the measurement of digital influence in *Klout Matters* and how you can position your business for it."

—Jeff Korhan, author of *Built-In Social*

"Read *Klout Matters* today to elevate and expand your business exponentially tomorrow."

—Holly Duckworth, CAE, CMP, and CEO of
Leadership Solutions International

"Finally, a book that opens the curtains on the influence that you and your brand actually have and what you can do to increase your impact."

—Shelle Rose Charvet, author of *Words That Change Minds*

"Buy this book! If you have something important to share, you will know how and why your own personal Klout matters . . . and what to do about it!"

—Dennis McCuistion, host and producer of the *McCuistion* program on PBS and executive director of the Institute for Excellence in Corporate Governance of the University of Texas at Dallas

"If you don't know what your Klout score is—or how to raise it—you need to read this book. Five stars out of five."

—Craig Rispin, CSP, speaker, and author of *How to Think Like a Futurist*

"Whenever I have questions, queries, or quandaries about the Internet or social media, I immediately revert to the lessons I have learned from Terry Brock and Gina Carr. Now they have packaged the secrets of their successes in *Klout Matters*. WOW! What a fantastic resource."

—Max Hitchins, "The Hospitality Doctor" and author of *The Hospitality Jungle*

"Get this book and read it before you get Klouted by all your competitors."

—Janelle Barlow, PhD, president of TMI US and former president of Global Speakers Federation

"Terry Brock and Gina Carr reveal insider tips and tricks for raising your Klout score. This is a must-read for anyone serious about social media in business."

—Dan Poynter, author of *Dan Poynter's Self-Publishing Manual*

"In *Klout Matters*, Terry Brock and Gina Carr teach you how to increase your connection to your tribe or communities through social media and improve your position as a thought leader."

—Cheryl Cran, CSP, author of *101 Ways to Make Generations X, Y, and Zoomers Happy at Work*

"From beginner to advanced practitioner, this book is a must-read if you are looking to influence others."

—Chad Hymas, CSP, CPAE, member of the National Speakers Association Hall of Fame, and author of *Doing What Must Be Done*

"A blueprint to leverage Klout for massive social influence, impact, and relationship capital. Read it—you need it!"

—Rob Brown, founder of Global Networking Council
and author of *How to Build Your Reputation*

"Buy, read and apply *Klout Matters* to make your clout matter."

—Phillip Van Hooser, author of *Leaders Ought to Know*

"*Klout Matters* will help any thought leader, industry expert, and business build their relationships and their brand success."

—Laura Rubinstein, cofounder of Social Buzz Club

"In this powerful book, Terry Brock and Gina Carr show you, step-by-step, exactly how to master Klout and reap its many benefits."

—Don Cooper, The Sales Heretic™

"*Klout Matters* is an indispensable tool for maximizing your success. If you are truly serious about taking your business to the next level, buy this book!"

—Steve Rizzo, author of *Get Your SHIFT Together*

"A must-read by two incredibly knowledgeable and skilled thought leaders."

—Carol Dodsley, the GPlus How2Girl

"In *Klout Matters*, Terry Brock and Gina Carr demystify Klout and emphasize that engagement, authenticity, and trustworthiness are the foundations for any social media strategy. Brock and Carr will show you how incorporating all of these raises your Klout score and increases your credibility."

—Ann Zuccardy, president of AZ Communications and
author of *A Brain Rebooted*

"If you understand that your ability to influence is critical to your success as a thought leader, entrepreneur, or businessperson, then you must read *Klout Matters*. Carr and Brock give you a roadmap with numerous strategies and tips for increasing your influence and relevance."

—Kathy Zader, president of Zoom Strategies

"Finally, an understandable guide to implementing the power of Klout in your marketing plan! If you're serious about making your online social presence really matter, you simply must read this book."

—Kit Grant, CSP, author of *Customer Service—Who Really Cares?*

"Gina Carr and Terry Brock lift the lid on how you can increase your online influence—and your business. Buy this book, read it, and do exactly what Gina and Terry advise. You'll be glad you did!"

—Simon Hazeldine, author of *Neuro-Sell*

"These two dynamos offer great resources to help you boost your business and your Klout score."

—Diane Bogino, president of Performance Strategies, Inc.

"*Klout Matters* is the most authoritative source on how to be influential in social media that I've seen."

—Dave Lieber, columnist at *The Dallas Morning News*

"Gina and Terry provide insightful ideas on how to use social media to engage customers more effectively, build more meaningful connections, and grow your business—all by raising your Klout score."

— Tim and Kris O'Shea, corporate keynote speakers

"If you care about your business, your influence and, your bottom line, *Klout Matters* is a must-read. Highly recommended!"

—Joy Ragan, author of *Divorce with Joy*

"A rich, practical how-to guide that even the social media novice can understand."

—Linda Byars Swindling, JD, CSP, author of
Stop Complainers and Energy Drainers

"Wow! If you're a thought leader, business leader, entrepreneur, or forward-thinking employee who wants to increase your influence and authority in a crowded and cluttered online world, this is a must-read. As a consultant who works with people who want to leverage their expertise and authority, I'm always looking for valuable resources on this topic to share with my clients—and this is one of the best."

—Gihan Perera, social media expert and author of *Fast, Flat, and Free*

KLOUT MATTERS

How to Engage Customers, Boost Your Digital Influence— and Raise Your Klout Score for Success

GINA CARR

and

TERRY BROCK

New York Chicago San Francisco Athens London Madrid Mexico City
Milan New Delhi Singapore Sydney Toronto

1 2 3 4 5 6 7 8 9 0   QFR/QFR   1 8 7 6 5 4 3

ISBN: 978-0-07-182731-7
MHID: 0-07-182731-5

e-ISBN: 978-0-07-182732-4
e-MHID: 0-07-182732-3

Gina Carr and Terry Brock have no affiliation with Klout. They believe in the work that Klout is doing to help people throughout the world become more influential.

Library of Congress Cataloging-in-Publication Data
Carr, Gina.
  Klout matters : how to engage customers, boost your digital influence : and raise your klout score for success / Gina Carr, Terry Brock.—1 Edition.
    pages cm
  ISBN-13: 978-0-07-182731-7
  ISBN-10: 0-07-182731-5
  1. Electronic commerce—Social aspects. 2. Influence (Psychology) 3. Persuasion (Psychology) 4. Internet marketing—Social aspects. 5. Social media—Economic aspects.
  I. Brock, Terry. II. Title.
  HF5548.32.C3625 2013
  658.8'72019—dc23
                              2013021926

To thought leaders around the world who create
compelling content to improve our lives,
a salute to you as we lift our fingers (momentarily)
off our keyboards to commend you on your brilliant work
that keeps us going!

Contents

Acknowledgments   vii

Foreword by Jeffrey Hayzlett   ix

Introduction   1

CHAPTER 1   What Is a Klout Score?   13

CHAPTER 2   Who Is Using Klout, and Who Should Care About It?   21

CHAPTER 3   Creating Content That Connects with Customers to Improve Your Klout Score   25

CHAPTER 4   Does Your Klout Score Really Matter?   29

CHAPTER 5   Should You Make an Effort to Increase Your Klout Score?   33

CHAPTER 6   What About Gaming the System?   41

CHAPTER 7   The Role of Vendors and Perks   51

CHAPTER 8   What You Can Do When You Don't Have Time for Social Media   69

CHAPTER 9   Tools That Can Help You Manage Social Media   93

CHAPTER 10   Enhance Your Social Media Presence— and Boost Your Klout Score!   99

CHAPTER 11   Getting Started with Klout   117

CHAPTER 12   Using Twitter to Raise Your Klout Score   123

CHAPTER 13   Using Facebook to Raise Your Klout Score   133

CHAPTER 14   Using LinkedIn to Raise Your Klout Score   147

CHAPTER 15 Using Other Networks to Raise Your Klout Score   153

CHAPTER 16 Online Collaborative Networks   159

CHAPTER 17 Myths About Boosting Your Klout Score   165

CHAPTER 18 What Klout Doesn't Count, but We Wish It Did!   171

CHAPTER 19 Whom Should You Engage With?   179

CHAPTER 20 So What Is a Thought Leader to Do?   189

APPENDIX A Podcasts We Recommend   193

APPENDIX B YouTube and Other Videos We Recommend   195

APPENDIX C Blogs We Recommend   198

APPENDIX D Resources for Building Your Business   203

Notes   206

Index   212

Acknowledgments

"None of us is not as smart as all of us."
—JAPANESE PROVERB

No work of this magnitude can be done alone. We are most grateful to the wonderful people who made this possible. We salute you and thank you for what you have done to help us, and, subsequently, the many people who will read and benefit from this book.

In particular, we would like to thank our wise and wonderful role models and friends Dianna Booher, Randy Gage, and Sam Horn. Without their inspiration, encouragement, and guidance, this book would not have become a reality.

Thanks also to the terrific folks at McGraw-Hill who saw the concept, believed in us, and helped shepherd us through the process, especially Stephanie Frerich and Casey Ebro.

Special thanks to marketing geniuses Jeffrey Gitomer, Jeffrey Hayzlett, and Harvey Mackay for their continued support, wisdom, and guidance.

The folks at Klout were most gracious in allowing us to visit their inspiring headquarters and become Kloutlaws for the day. We gained great insight into what Klout is all about and what it will become by meeting with several of the top leaders: CEO and cofounder Joe Fernandez, cofounder Binh Tran, Director of People and Culture Katelin Holloway, VP of Marketing Paul Kim, Director of Business Development Jon Dick, Head of Communications Lynn Fox, Community Manager Sahana Ullagaddi, and Chief Scientist Ding Zhou. Thank you for providing an insider's look at how you are pioneering the social scoring industry. We look forward to watching your creation blossom and grow.

We interviewed and surveyed several marketing experts, who contributed tips, tools, and strategies: Kare Anderson, Jay Baer, Amanda Blain, Bob Burg, Michelle Colon-Johnson, Joel Comm, Mark Fidelman, Jane Garee, Kim Garst, J.B. Glossinger, Debbie Horovitch, Lisa Jimenez, Mary Kelly, Dwayne Kilbourne, Judson Laipply, Heather Lutze, Edel O'Mahony, Winston Marsh, Joachim de Posada, Srinivas Rao, Kathryn Rose, Kimberly Reynolds, Viveka von Rosen, Laura Rubinstein, Mark Schaefer, Gina Schreck, Mari Smith, Alan Stevens, Bruce Turkel, Carly Alyssa Thorne, and Andrea Vahl. (If we've omitted anyone, we offer sincere apologies. Please reach out and let us know. We'll make amends.)

Gina owes particular gratitude to longtime special friends who have provided love, encouragement, and support through the years: Ita Doré, Cindy Nora Hart, Felicia McAleer, the late Muriel Mabry Tempero, Cheryl Johnson Weldon, and Mary Wilhite.

To Crystal Carr and Thomas Carr, you are the best siblings a girl could ever ask for. Thanks for always being there for me (Gina).

To the late Thomas Carr, Charles Brock, and Donald Kyle, we thank you for all you did to make us the people we are today.

Most of all, thanks to our wonderful mothers, Patsy Brock and Billie Carr, who have guided us, loved us, encouraged us, and consoled us through the ups and downs of life.

And to all the people we have the privilege of knowing and being with through the years, we salute you and appreciate you. Thank you for making our lives better!

Foreword

BY JEFFREY HAYZLETT,
GLOBAL BUSINESS CELEBRITY AND BESTSELLING AUTHOR
OF *MIRROR TEST* AND *RUNNING THE GAUNTLET*

Working with companies across the globe, I've heard business people claim social media doesn't do anything for their business; it isn't important and is a waste of time. WRONG! It's obvious social media is here to stay. From Main Street to Wall Street, almost every brand and every company have at least a Facebook page or a Twitter handle. And every event I speak at has a social component with Twitter, texting, and more.

Consumers are connected to their brands 24/7 through social media. Because of that, they expect to be acknowledged, listened to, and in some cases, see action. You can't afford to only do business from nine to five anymore. We've seen the aftermath of brands that fail to respond to the social media messages of their customers and stakeholders. We've also seen brands win the day because of their response time and impeccable engagement.

There is a new currency for brands, be they corporate or personal. That currency is about relevancy, intent, and influence. And it's measurable. Digital influence is a testament to great relationships and great content. To put it simply, it's no longer only about who you know, but also how you engage with who you know. How do brands drive action through social media? How do marketers measure the results? One way is via a person or company's influencer score. Digital influence will come to us in many names like the one these authors have written so wonderfully about. Influence defines your credibility.

This means relationships and trust are more important than ever. Who are you more likely to believe? The marketing team behind a great product or your best friend? More than likely, you're going to trust your friend. I coined the term "friendsourcing" for this strategy, and it's all about the power of social influence.

From the great minds of my friends Gina Carr and Terry Brock comes *Klout Matters*. They've packaged their experience and expertise into a book that provides the ins and outs of your digital influence score—which translates to your ability to gain the trust of others. As a social media maverick myself, I found the advice, tips, and tricks given in this book helpful to any who want to improve their own score and their overall standing in the social media world.

Your influencer score is more than just a number. It is a quantifiable way to show others you know your social stuff. These scores are now being used to qualify job candidates, define invitation lists, prove status, and other measures of "worthiness." But the real beauty is that in the past, you needed to be a celebrity to be considered influential. Now, anyone with a computer, social networks, and solid engaging content can become an influential expert in his or her field.

Social media is crucial for me in business. In fact, many of my leads come through friendsourcing and being online and transparent with my followers. Transparency is key. Being an influencer doesn't mean you can get away with sharing crappy information and updating every once in a while. Have a personality and keep giving your followers and fans things to make them come back and check in. Be real with them! Be radically transparent and share with them not only your business, but a piece of you as well.

A real cowboy knows you have to be able to really ride the trail. Carr and Brock will be our guides on this ride and show us the way to be the best influencers we can be. So get ready, it's time to saddle up and ride.

Introduction

Klout digs deep into social media to understand how people influence each other, so that everyone can discover and be recognized for how they influence the world.
—FROM KLOUT WEBSITE

What's your Klout Score? A few short years ago (before 2008) that question would generate faces with twisted expressions wondering what you were talking about. People would also let you know you spell it with a *c*, not a *k*.

Times have changed.

Today, Klout is the dominant system of grading and rating how much influence people have based on a mysterious alchemy of numeric calculations. This seems like wizardry, but the people at Klout have some pretty scientific algorithms to determine what they claim is an individual's or brand's Klout Score. It has become one of the hottest buzzwords in the social media world.

While doing research for this book, we made a personal visit to the Klout headquarters in San Francisco, California. One of the interviews we had was with Joe Fernandez, the cofounder and CEO of Klout. He encapsulated where we are today when he said, "The Internet is moving from being centered around pages to centered around people." You can see a video of the interview we had with Joe Fernandez by going to http://KloutMatters.com/videos-and-more or scanning the QR code that follows on page 2 with your smartphone.

A few years ago, the focus was on having a web page and knowledge of how to navigate around and get information from the Internet. Today, the emphasis is on social media. Businesspeople are expected to have a strong working knowledge of social media and why it's important to get hired for many positions. Those who deal with the

ideas, thoughts, words, and concepts need to have especially strong skills with various social media platforms.

In this book, we are going to take a journey into what a Klout Score is, why it is important to some—but not everyone—and what you can do about yours. You'll hear from proponents of Klout as well as the detractors. You'll be able to make up your own mind and take action based on what is right for you, your business, and your career.

Reliable data is important when making decisions. Today buyers more and more want to make decisions based on what the most influential people are saying about a given brand or other topic. For instance, if an employer has to decide between two equally qualified candidates for a job, they often look for some quantitative measure to help break the tie, such as your Klout Score. A Klout Score provides a way to determine who is more influential than another in terms of social media, and this score has become the criterion often used as a tiebreaker when a decision has to be made between two equally qualified candidates for a given role.

The old concept of only going on your gut feeling is rapidly eroding and being replaced by measurement and analysis. More and more quantitative analysis is being used to determine social influence. Klout collects over 12 billion data points per day along with 400 signals on seven networks, making Klout and big data inextricably linked.[1]

Defining Klout

Klout is a social scoring system that is similar to a credit score or the BMI (body mass index). It is used to measure your online and offline influence in various ways. Klout's website describes how the score is calculated in general terms:

The majority of the signals used to calculate the Klout Score are derived from combinations of attributes, such as the ratio of reactions you generate compared to the amount of content you share. For example, generating 100 retweets from 10 tweets will contribute more to your Score than generating 100 retweets from 1,000 tweets. We also consider factors such as how selective the people who interact with your content are. The more a person likes and retweets in a given day, the less each of those individual interactions contributes to another person's score. Additionally, we value the engagement you drive from unique individuals. One-hundred retweets from 100 different people contribute more to your Score than do 100 retweets from a single person.[2]

Klout was founded by Joe Fernandez and Binh Tran in 2008. Joe Fernandez had been looking for a way to quantify influence. In 2007, Joe had surgery that required his jaw to be wired shut. Everything he ate had to be strained, even soup, so that he could digest it. During that healing process, he couldn't talk and was limited to using his typing skills to communicate with others, largely through social media sites like Twitter and Facebook. It was during that time that he realized how important it was to connect with key influencers on the net, and from that realization, the idea of Klout was born.

Since its humble beginnings, Klout has grown to be recognized worldwide as a way to determine the amount of influence someone has.

Many brands are interested in Klout now because it gives them a way to identify those who are most influential within a given community. Rather than spreading their advertising dollars across a variety of media, using "spray and pray" marketing, now brands can be more effective and efficient when spending their marketing dollars.

Using what we like to call advocate marketing, brands can take advantage of the influence that someone has and leverage that persuasive power. We like to define advocate marketing as "the practice of a brand getting exposure by leveraging the talent, recognition, and influence of another to promote its product and/or services." This has been done for years through spokespeople for various brands. The advocate does the marketing more effectively than the brand.

Today, Klout and other social media influence scoring companies have established a rapidly evolving system where they identify key people who are influential in a given community, then forge a relationship with that person who can speak more objectively about the product or service of the brand. The concept of "advocate marketing" is often the most effective for the brand and most believable for the end user.

The metaphor that keeps coming to our minds when we think about Klout is one that reminds us of social media and the confusion that surrounds it. Imagine yourself at sea in a small rowboat several miles from shore while it is very dark at night and a huge storm is raging about you. You are being tossed to and fro wondering what to do and sometimes even wondering if you will make it back to shore.

Social media can be much like that.

The social media landscape is changing constantly like that stormy sea. Every day, your challenge is to do more on more platforms with less and less time available. Often you see the competition doing something unique and brilliant and you feel even more despondent. As the waves of turbulent waters knock around a little rowboat at sea, you could feel tossed about in the fast-moving world of social media.

We see Klout as the light from a lighthouse on shore. That lighthouse will give you a goal and a direction that you can follow to reach safety. Klout does not require you to perform a certain set of tasks. Instead, Klout provides guidance that you can use to build your business, increase your digital influence—and yes, increase your Klout Score.

Some might wonder why a Klout Score even matters. In our research, we found many people questioning why they would need to care at all about something like a Klout Score.

A popular article in *Wired* magazine received a lot of attention when it profiled an individual, Sam Fiorella, who was looking for a job in the marketing industry. When interviewed for a marketing position, Fiorella didn't know his Klout Score—34 at the time—and he lost the job to someone who had a Klout Score of 67.[3]

Social media is full of too many charlatans who are touting a "secret new way" to raise your Klout Score. Too often these are based on questionable and less-than-ethical tricks. Success over the long term requires practicing the very principles that are recommended by

Klout to raise your Klout Score. If you keep an eye on those recommendations, that beacon in the storm, you will succeed now and in the long term.

While adults no longer play on the playground (at least not often!), those playground politics and who the "cool" kids are still exists in most business circles. We're concerned with status and want to be liked; we might even want to be the most popular person. So placing a specific numbered score, which changes daily, on people about how "cool" or influential they are is bound to get people riled up.

If you are a thought leader, run a business or brand, want a better job, or even just to get free stuff online and have brands listen to you more, this book is for you. *Klout Matters* will help you improve not only your Klout Score but your business, career, and influence as well. Measurements like Klout can help you strengthen your business strategies and even your personal brand. While this book talks about how to raise your Klout Score, it also focuses on what to do to increase your business and influence online. Think of it as a double benefit to you. By following the practices we suggest and applying the technologies we discuss, you will increase your business and influence, which will in turn lead to a higher Klout Score! These time-honored principles, combined with cutting-edge technology, are part of the recipe behind increasing your score. You also have a greater chance of getting more business as you regularly and consistently embrace better practices.

A Klout Score is a measure of how influential a person is online. Klout doesn't just track how many tweets people have sent or how many friends or fans they have on Facebook. It is a deeper analysis of how effective they are at motivating others to take action. This means that people do something as a result of what the person has suggested, recommended, or placed online.

An example of this would be a retweet on Twitter. If people read your tweet on Twitter and enjoy what you said, they can retweet your tweet, which means their followers will be able to see what you wrote, sometimes with added comments. Being retweeted means that you have influence, and Klout takes this into account when measuring your score. The goal is not necessarily to get more followers, since this doesn't affect your Klout Score. The goal is to initiate action on the part of others.

Those who have the most influence are the people who have higher Klout Scores. The more you can move people to take some specific form of action (like a retweet), the more influential you are perceived to be by the Klout measuring techniques.

This matters a great deal to cash-strapped businesses today. Instead of pouring a great deal of their budget into traditional media like radio, television, and print publications, they are likely to get a bigger bang for their buck focusing on key influencers or advocates. Many brands today are asking influencers to evaluate their products and then to talk about them in their blog posts, podcasts, YouTube videos, and other places online. Many businesses have found their money is much better spent working with key influencers than trying to blast a message to a mass market.

Some parallels can be seen between today and the early days of search engine marketing when it comes to measuring digital influence. In 1998 and 1999, Google was the most important search engine around. Yet, what Google did in 1999 pales in comparison to what it offers today. Google has not only improved its search engine algorithms, but it has also added many other services that are beneficial to consumers.

In the same way, we are in the beginning stages of digital influence measurement. Klout, and its competitors like Kred, PeerIndex, Appinions, and many others, are in the beginning stages of truly measuring digital influence. Much excitement is centered around this new era when we can more effectively measure someone's true influence by correct quantitative analysis rather than by a traditional "gut feeling." The concept of big data is with us now and growing stronger, and Klout is intricately tied to big data.

As noted statistician and writer Nate Silver put it, "Every day, three times per second, we produce the equivalent of the amount of data that the Library of Congress has in its entire print collection. Most of it is . . . irrelevant noise. So unless you have good techniques for filtering and processing the information, you're going to get into trouble."[4]

To determine a Klout Score, the algorithms used rely on over 12 billion pieces of data every day to determine how influential a given person is. In a conversation with Ding Zhou, the chief scientist at Klout, we realized that big data is an integral part of what the company is doing. Klout is using massive amounts of information to understand what is going on in the world and thereby arrive at a reasonably accurate Klout Score. We say "reasonably accurate" because even Klout's scientists admit that they're not perfect and that they are constantly working to make the process more refined and better all around.

This is especially important today for those deciding who they want to associate with, hire, or work with based on what is really happening in the marketplace.

Decision makers for brands and for hiring decisions have looked for a more quantifiable, measurable tool by which to make decisions. Klout is the leader in this relatively new field. When a meeting planner has to decide which speaker to use for an upcoming convention, a quantifiable metric can help to make that decision. A key factor in this process, particularly in the mind of the meeting planner, is to make sure not to make a bad decision. Klout provides a system and an ultimately easy, measurable number by which decision makers can decide who to hire.

This applies to brands as well. How can you cut through all of the hype in the market to find out who it is that you need to connect with on a regular basis? Who can be the most influential and effective endorser of your brand? It's all about developing relationships with the right people. To find out who the right people are, Klout is an instrumental tool.

Today's astute thought leaders know that metrics in social media are important. On a panel at New Media Expo in January 2013, held in Las Vegas, Nevada, Eric Kuhn and David Tochterman, two marketers who are social media savvy, talked about the importance of social metrics. They both indicated that in screenings today, producers and directors of major motion pictures are looking at a whole package of variables to decide which talent to use. They were asked about the importance of the Klout Score for selecting actors.[5] Eric Kuhn said, "If you have 100,000 followers and a Klout Score of 74, that's intriguing." He went on to say, "You don't get the job because you have that, but it is more and more becoming a factor."

If Hollywood producers and directors are considering Klout Scores, it is something that any thought leader, business owner, brand manager, or individual working on a personal brand needs to consider today. It will be a factor considered even more in the future. We have a strong need today to make decisions based on quantitative metrics, not just relying only on one's intuition.

Eric Kuhn was later asked what a respectable Klout Score is, and he said, "60, 70, 80. 40? Try a little harder."

This is the reality of our world today. You might not like it, but in the end, decision makers are considering Klout Scores and similar metrics as a critical factor for hiring talent and promoting their products directly to influencers. If you are in a field like content creation, entertainment, professional speaking, or other service-related industries, you need to be aware of your Klout Score.

Klout, Kred, PeerIndex, Appinions, and other influence measurement tools help you sort the "chaff from the wheat." These tools attempt to measure the amount of real influence that someone has. By making the process more quantitative and objective, the goal is that it will be much more accurate. This requires accumulation of large amounts of data. This topic is what is now called, "big data," and it involves another major trend in the field of analytics. More and more data is collected on a variety of topics. When large-scale computers can crunch massive amounts of numbers and data (well into the petabytes of information, trillions of data points), they can come up with previously unseen correlations. The process of accumulating information is being used by Klout to continually refine and improve on its measurement.

Part of this accumulation of data relates to search engine technology. In September 2012, Microsoft, Bing, and Klout formed a partnership. Klout Scores will be affected by the amount of searches on specific names. For instance, if a particular celebrity is searched more often on Bing, that can affect that celebrity's Klout Score.

Microsoft and Klout are sharing information so that Klout data will be incorporated into Bing and Klout Scores will begin to take Bing search results into account. The relationship, as it was formed, is only the beginning and will have profound effects on determining influence. When you combine the benefits of big data that is used in a search on Bing and the algorithms to determine influence, it has many possibilities.

People might try to game the system by bumping their score through likes or +Ks that someone can give. However, it is a lot harder, even impossible, to persuade millions of people to search for someone. We are only in the beginning stages of this reality, but it has great possibilities.

With this sharing of data, Klout Scores will reflect searches, which are a component in influence. At least with Bing (it is yet to be determined if Google will enter a similar agreement with Klout), searches can be used as a valid ingredient in the mix to calculate a score. This goes far beyond just analyzing or enhancing one's Klout Score, yet it shows the value of understanding what is involved with quantitative measurement with tools like Klout.

Much of the criticism of influence scoring is based on reality. For instance, a recent study showed people having influence in Japanese earthquakes only because they retweeted information about Japanese earthquakes. Just because people retweet a topic does not mean that they have the authority to be able to talk about that subject from a credible point of view. Someone can be an avid fan or devotee of a particular topic; however, that does not make that person an authority. In this book we will show the importance of going deeper to analyze the true influence and authority that a person has.

Klout is now starting to factor in offline influential factors. This would include such important considerations as job experience, formal education, and other areas that contribute to one's authority. If someone is listed in Wikipedia, they usually have a lot of credibility. Wikipedia calls this "noteable." If someone has a Wikipedia page, they will have a good chance of having a higher Klout Score than another person with comparable credentials and background. A Klout Score is also calculated by contextual references to people in the *New York Times*. This process of using offline, real-world sources will increase in the future as Klout further refines and enhances its algorithms.

For instance, in the profession of public speaking, we have seen many people who claim to be "the world's greatest motivational speaker." But think of it from the point of view of an event planner looking to book the speaker: how do you know who is "the best" and the most suitable match for your event? You can watch speakers' reels, research online, ask around, and more, but a Klout Score already offers that extra tool to help weigh in on outside influence. Remember, when human beings are involved in making a decision, logic is not the only tool used.

The late, great Zig Ziglar said that we make our decisions with emotion and then lock them in with logic. One's clout (yes, with a *c*) has always been an important consideration in choosing which person to believe or select for service. Today, Klout (with a *K*) is a significant factor in making decisions and falls more on the logical, analytical side than on the emotional side. We contend that it is one factor that should be considered in making a decision, but not the only factor.

As with most situations in life, the answer is not a simple, straightforward one. The true answer is developed through a series of questions digging deeper and doing further analysis. In this book, we will show you some tools that can help you make better decisions on booking vendors who offer professional services. If you provide professional services, you will find a lot of specific help to guide you through the maze of social influence.

We will pay particular attention to, and give advice to, thought leaders. These are the wonderful people around the world who communicate with us through speeches, writing, coaching, facilitating, and consulting. They are more reliant on social media than others are.

We like the way Jeff Bullas, a blogger and thought leader himself, from Sydney, Australia, puts it: "Thought leadership is not ordinary content but rather content that sets one brand apart from the competition and, in the process, leverages a phenomenal platform for trust and engagement."[6] The content that thought leaders generate helps them to stand out with a message that is unique and compelling.

Mari Smith is widely known as one of the world's leading experts on marketing with Facebook and other social media platforms. When she talks about content and engagement in social media, she says it well:

> *Content is King, but engagement is Queen . . . and she rules the house! You might manage to set up automated and delegated content dissemination systems, but if you're not engaging with your fans and followers on a daily basis, you're missing the other half of the equation. Engagement builds social equity.*[7]

Most of this book is based on the nuts and bolts of how you can perform certain activities that will help you increase business in the social media world. As you focus on those activities that help you connect with people, you are more likely to have your Klout Score raised.

We'll look at who is using Klout and how it is generating serious, real-world benefits in business. Is it for everyone? No, but for those who can benefit from using it, you have to pay attention. For marketers, professional speakers, and other influencers, it is imperative to know about it and determine what the right approach is for each person.

In this book, we'll also examine how you can use various tools to calculate your score. We'll get "under the hood" with Twitter to find out the most effective way to generate buzz—and hence a higher Klout Score. We'll look at the giant of social media, Facebook. We'll also go in-depth with tools like LinkedIn, Foursquare, Wikipedia, Google+, and more, all of which serve as platforms to affect your Klout Score. What activities should a thought leader engage in to yield the best results?

We'll also share those areas that currently don't affect your Klout Score, but many think should. These would include YouTube, blogs, and other areas.

Since we know that you are pressed for time, we'll focus a healthy amount of attention on how you can best manage the time it takes to "do" social media and how that affects your Klout Score. We'll learn from some prominent thought leaders who use social media and leverage a high Klout Score into serious bottom-line business.

You'll get some specific insights into what is the right strategy for you and have a checklist to make your efforts at boosting your Klout Score pay off.

Most important, we're not just going to focus on what you need to do to raise your Klout Score, but what you need to do to generate more business as well. Yes, it is nice to boost your Klout Score, but it is only valid if it leads to more business. We are both entrepreneurs and understand the time pressures and budget constraints that exist for serious business leaders, but we also understand the importance of your Klout Score.

Get ready for an objective, hard-hitting analysis of what Klout is all about, if you should worry about it, and how you can boost your score. You'll meet a lot of influential people and find out what they are doing to boost their own Klout Score (if they care). You'll also learn about some inside tricks that can boost your Klout Score and determine if that is right for you.

One of the fun challenges we have in writing about social media and a fast-moving company like Klout is that as soon as we finish writing this book, there will be changes in the environment. We like the analogy that David Perlmutter of the University of Iowa uses that writing about blogging is like writing about NASCAR on stone tablets. The pace is changing so fast, you need something different to keep up with it all![8] To accomplish that end, we have created a website and Facebook page specifically for you, the reader of this book: http://KloutMatters.com. You'll be able to go there for updates and to interact with other readers. This way we can keep you updated with changes to this subject matter.

We look forward to having you on the journey. Fasten your seat belt. Your wonderful journey into building your Klout Score—and increasing your business—is about to begin!

–Terry Brock and Gina Carr

P.S.: Although this book has an ending, the fun is just beginning! Join us at http://www.KloutMatters.com for more tips, tools, newly released video interviews, course offerings, and additional resources. We look forward to seeing you and welcoming you into our tribe!

CHAPTER 1

What Is a Klout Score?

Klout digs deep into social media to understand how people influence each other, so that everyone can discover and be recognized for how they influence the world.
—KLOUT WEBSITE

Klout is a system that has been devised, and continues to undergo regular refinement, to analyze and measure the degree of a person's influence.

In sum, if your work relates to influencing others to take action, then you should pay attention to Klout. Is it for everyone? Not quite. However, if you work as a professional speaker, coach, consultant, facilitator, author, entertainer, blogger, podcaster, or in any other profession where you influence others, you need to pay attention to Klout. These thought leaders are people who have always exerted a certain amount of influence over others. In the past one's degree of influence was always open to subjectivity. It still is today, even with the use of Klout.

However, the difference today is that Klout has been developed so that we can more accurately measure what was only subjective before. By using sophisticated computer algorithms, the people at Klout have been able to ascertain more of what one's true influence is by looking at what happens with others over several different platforms and applications.

As an example, many people can say that Joe Speaker is very influential. But the important question is, "How does one know the true extent of influence that Joe Speaker really exerts?" There are some who would say Joe is exceptionally influential, whereas others would say Joe Speaker is not influential. In the past, without Klout, it was a matter of opinion. People relied more on their "gut feeling."

Today it still is opinion because influence is very subjective even with the most sophisticated algorithms. Joe Speaker could be highly influential for one group of people and have zero influence over others.

Klout is a system by which you can more reliably gauge the accuracy of influence, at least by certain measured criteria. We can still debate how influential Joe Speaker is among ourselves. However, when you can show that Joe has moved certain people to action on Facebook, on Twitter, and on other platforms, this indicates that Joe Speaker has a degree of influence that needs to be addressed.

Of course, if you are Joe Speaker and you feel that you have a lot of influence, you naturally want and expect your Klout Score to be high. Having been in the professional speaking community for over 30 years, we have yet to find a speaker whose ego doesn't make the speaker feel that he or she deserves a higher score! Probably that is just the nature of strong-ego professional speakers!

But let's move the focus away from the individual speaker or influencer. If you are marketing a brand and are looking to connect with someone who is highly influential in a given community, you want to make sure that there is a more objective way of measuring that person's influence. Just listening to two or three people say, "Joe Speaker is highly influential" is not enough. If you're going to pay for an endorsement from Joe, you want to know that he can significantly influence people in a given market.

This is why Klout has emerged so prominently. There is a market that needs to know who is more influential than others. With social media so prominent in our world today, many people want to find out more objectively who exerts the most influence over others in a given field.

Of course, any measuring system is going to draw fire from those who are not rated as highly as they think they should be. It is also going to draw fire from those who like to be at the center of attention by complaining and being the snarky outsider-attacker against any system that is very popular. Journalists are particularly prone to do this. Terry has been a journalist for over 40 years writing for various publications—newspapers, magazines, and many blogs. Journalists by nature often try to find the "alternate point of view" in a given situation. You might say that journalists just want to raise their own Klout Scores, and a good way to do that is to gain attention by attacking the Klout system.

All that is just to say that it's important to "follow the money" (as the then-anonymous "Deep Throat" told us during the Watergate era). When you hear strong criticism of endorsement of a particular idea, it is always wise to "follow the money" to find out what is really happening. Is someone complaining about a new system or product because he or she wasn't selected to participate? Is it "sour grapes" because that person was turned down to serve in a particular position?

Klout is a system that attempts to help people understand who is most influential in a given area. It has emerged and is successful because people desire this kind of objective rating.

Think of it like the FICO scores that were developed in the banking community to better determine who is creditworthy and who is not. FICO scores were developed by Fair Isaac Corporation to be a more objective way of determining loan-worthy applicants.

A useful benefit of a FICO score can be that if yours is lower than you wanted it to be, you know specific tasks you can undertake to raise that score. By undertaking the tasks that are required to raise your FICO score, you are doing what is important to be more creditworthy and be more financially sound.

The criticism that has been raised about the Klout Score is that it is not quite the same as a FICO score or BMI. Regardless of what you think of about FICO scores or BMI, it is fairly well known what factors go into the calculation of the algorithm so you can address those to improve your own individual score.

We particularly like the metaphor of looking at your Klout Score like your BMI (body mass index). For instance, if you have a BMI score that you don't want, there are many specific steps you can take, which are well known. You know to abstain from certain foods, to consume various alternate foods, to engage in a certain level of exercise, and to do other activities under the supervision of a competent healthcare professional.[1] Calculating your Klout Score is very much like calculating your BMI.

In a video interview we did while writing this book, we spoke with one of the gurus in the world of branding, Bruce Turkel of Turkel Brands. Bruce and his company work with companies like Bacardi,

Miami Tourism, HBO, Jackson Memorial Hospital, and many others. Before he even read this book, Bruce was using the same metaphor of the Klout Score being like your BMI. (Great minds think alike.) Bruce said, "Social media is really the first time you've had free, democratized access to distribution. With social media you can get your messages out in front of people you want to reach, and people you haven't thought of reaching yet."[2] You can view the entire educational video with Bruce at http://KloutMatters.com/videos-and-more.

As medical professionals continue to refine and improve the quality of a BMI score and as financial professionals tweak and modify the formulation for a FICO score, we know that those active in the digital influence world are continuing to improve their analyzing and rating methodology. We're in the embryonic stages of this area now. Those close to the industry like Joe Fernandez, CEO of Klout, and Andrew Grill, CEO of Klout's closest competitor, Kred, agree—we're just getting started.

The industry is off to a good start, and a lot of very smart people are bringing some sophisticated tools to bear on this important area of influence. It is an exciting playground to be in at this time in history!

Your Klout Score is going to be a reflection of the marketing and interaction with customers that you do in the right way. We recommend that you do not focus on your Klout Score. Focus instead on doing those activities that are naturally right for connecting with customers and making them "giddy with glee." Engage with customers. If you focus on doing what your customers want and how you can solve their problems, you will inevitably build your business. As you build your business, the natural outcome will be a higher and stronger Klout Score.

Engaging with customers is the key for success in the social media era. It has always been this way in business since rug traders operated in ancient Mesopotamia millennia ago.

However, in the world of social media today, we find it is more important than ever. People want to know real individuals, real people at companies with whom they are doing business. When employers are hiring someone for a thought leader position, they want to have someone who is influential. By engaging with customers and engaging with other key stakeholders, one's influence is naturally raised.

In the same way, it could be said that to raise one's FICO score would require engagement in certain healthy financial activities. For example, paying credit card bills on time and in full can help to raise one's FICO score. Engaging in activities that render you more credit-worthy and financially stable makes a lot of sense. These are not open to question, nor is the solution enshrouded in any esoteric mystery.

However, when it comes to determining one's Klout Score, a lot of esoteric mystery enshrouds the process. Many people will try to raise their Klout Score, doing what they feel are the right activities, only to be disappointed because they see their Klout Score has actually gone down. Understandably, this is why many people become very frustrated with their Klout Scores.

Klout is calculating over 12 billion data points in 400 key areas every day to determine an individual's Klout Score. That is far more data points than are considered in either a FICO credit score or a BMI for health. That makes the "how do they calculate the score?" question difficult, if not impossible, to answer. This parallels the development in the computer field known as big data, where massive amounts of information are collected, then analyzed to generate cause-and-effect relationships that were previously unrecognized.

Without mentioning any names, we both know people who became frustrated and "left the system" because their Klout Score wasn't what they wanted it to be. Their Klout Score went down when they tried to "behave" and do what is encouraged in the Klout system. Even if you disagree with their actions, one can understand why certain individuals would want to do the digital equivalent of "taking their bat and ball and going home."

Along these lines, many have expressed a desire to have a more open, visible, and transparent means of understanding how one's Klout Score is rated. To go back to our metaphors of BMI scores or FICO scores, it is fairly well known what one needs to do to improve either of these measurements. However, raising one's Klout Score often remains a rather elusive—and frustrating—experience.

The good people at Klout tell us that it is important to create compelling content to raise one's Klout Score. This is extraordinarily important. And without giving away all of our book in the first chapter (you must promise to continue reading here), we have to agree!

Creating compelling content in your niche is one of the most important ways that you can raise your Klout Score. It is sustainable. It is business savvy. It is the right thing to do.

Yet we have also found that merely creating compelling content is not enough, in and of itself, to create and maintain a higher Klout Score. Of course, that's why you need to keep reading this book!

It would be good for Klout to be more transparent in exposing what is in its "secret sauce." It would be nice to know that if one does X, Y, and Z, then one would be able to raise one's Klout Score by a certain number of points. We understand it is vastly complicated and requires a strong understanding of quantitative analysis to decipher even the rudimentary basics of how the actual score is calculated.

Unfortunately, if this formula were known and visible to people, it would encourage many to merely game the system. Many would try to get a higher Klout Score without performing the necessary tasks of engaging and connecting with customers properly.

We remember back in the early days of Internet marketing that many people would use certain tricks to try to get a higher Google ranking. People used tricks like putting keywords in the same color as the background of the page. For example, if the text was in black ink against a white background, these "SEO experts" would encourage people to enter keywords liberally throughout their web pages all in the same white as the white background. This would make the text invisible to the human eye, but machines would see it and give a higher SEO ranking to the page. Many people at Internet conferences would giggle and elbow each other, thinking that they had discovered a magic "secret way" to boost their SEO ranking and to game the Google system.

What happened back then, and what usually happens with these types of schemes, is that Google found out what was happening and quickly put an end to it. Think about it—the people at Google are not stupid. If their system is being abused, as they see it, they are going to try to stop such behavior.

Fast-forward to today. The people at Klout are going to behave in a similar way if they feel that their system is being abused. From time to time, you're going to read about "a cool new way to get a higher Klout Score" that is nothing more than gaming the system. Google was always on the lookout for these types of gaming systems, as is

Klout today. When those trying to game the system are found, dire consequences could happen to their Klout Score.

Yes, you might be able to boost your Klout Score a few points by using the latest cool gizmo and trick that is in the marketplace. However, such a system is not sustainable and does not help to build business in the long term.

And really, that's what it is all about. It is not about merely getting a higher Klout Score, but rather it is important and imperative to build a solid, sustainable business for the long term. It is our contention throughout this book that the emphasis of true thought leaders today should be on developing a sustainable business model by providing compelling content and engaging with customers in a genuine, caring way.

Randy Gage is a professional speaker, author, and now successful social media user. He stresses that the term is *social* media. It is not selling media or spam media but social.[3] You have to get to know people as people in a genuine, authentic way where you connect with them as people. You can listen to an interview we did with Randy Gage and learn more about how he has generated millions of dollars in revenue in the video that accompanies this book. It is available at http://KloutMatters.com/videos-and-more.

As we interviewed many successful social media users in preparing for this book, we discovered some very interesting patterns. They consistently emphasized being genuine and focused on helping others. This is basic material that you'll read about in any selling book worth its salt. In the realm of social media it is taken to an even higher level because of the ubiquitous nature of social media.

Bob Burg, professional speaker and coauthor of *The Go-Giver* and *Endless Referrals*, shared this with us in a video interview. He said that you need to "shift your focus from yourself to an 'other' focus."[4] You have to think about how you can help other people. This is true in life, and it is even more evident in social media as it can be monitored more clearly.

When Joe Fernandez developed Klout, he saw it as a way to find out who was most influential in a given area. Now it is imperative to find ways to build and prove that a business holds a long-term position of influence.

Long-term influence is what most thought leaders know they need to build. This is essential to remain in business and in a position as a thought leader. A sudden burst of energy that gives a momentary "flash in the pan" doesn't make a person a strong thought leader. True long-term influence requires ongoing and continually renewed effort to help others achieve their goals as you provide answers to their problems.

CHAPTER 2

Who Is Using Klout, and Who Should Care About It?

*I'll care about my Klout score when I get a
free surfboard in the mail.*
—SRINIVAS RAO, HOST AND COFOUNDER OF BLOGCASTFM

Ultimately what matters is the buyer. It does not matter what your Klout Score is unless that score matters to someone making a purchasing decision about you or your product. It also can matter among peers. If we know that Dr. Mary Smith is well known in nuclear physics and her knowledge is perceived as high value among her peers, then her score would be important to those in the field of nuclear physics.

Many would say that what matters most is what buyers consider an influential person. If Klout is using a different score and doesn't rank someone as high, it doesn't necessarily mean that person would not get any business. If a buyer considers someone credible and wants to do business with that person, then one's Klout Score is not quite as important.

A Klout Score is a determinant among those who have little or no knowledge of others in a given field. For instance, if you are looking for a person who is an expert in the field of archaeology, and you don't know many archaeologists, finding those archaeologists who have a higher Klout Score could be a good place to start. If someone has been rated as a good archaeologist by other people in that field, then that would be beneficial to know before hiring an archaeologist.

Many potential employers today are considering a Klout Score before they hire someone. This has profound ramifications for those who are looking for jobs. In a very tight economy where jobs are in high demand, it is important to do whatever you can to stand out from your peers. It is easy to sit back, cross your arms, and say that a Klout Score doesn't really matter. However, if you're in the market to get a job, or get a particular assignment, and those who are buying your product value a high Klout Score, then you need to pay attention to it!

Todd Bacile is a professor of marketing and business at Florida State University. He says that people need to focus on Klout, not because they think it is important, but because others do.[1]

Ryan Thornburg is a professor at USC who uses the Klout Score as 20 percent of a student's grade.[2] How is that possibly fair to students who are struggling to raise this arbitrary number that's contrived inside a black box? It's fair because it transforms the class from a workshop on button pushing to an exercise in hypothesis testing, strategy, and critical thinking. Students—who often approach grades with calculating economy of effort—don't know what they have to do to boost their Klout Scores, so they are forced to design simple experiments, isolate variables, and generalize their findings.[3]

This theory makes a lot of sense. You have to pay attention to what others value—not just what you consider valuable. Dr. Bacile uses this in his classroom because students in his classes are going to be judged by their Klout Score when they enter the job market. Bacile's reasoning is that since students' Klout Scores will be a factor in their lives after graduation, it makes sense to use it before graduation. Therefore he is using students' Klout Scores as a component in the overall grade mix.

Other people today can rant that a given score doesn't matter. What does matter, however, is what other people consider important. The old phrase of "What is important is what important people consider to be important" still holds true today. When important people regard your Klout Score as important, it pays to pay attention!

When Gina was a student at Harvard Business School, getting her MBA, a big part of the grade was participation in class. Active participation is still a component of one's grade at Harvard Business School today.

This is true with Klout. Active participation is important for a strong Klout Score. Of course, Klout is not the only measure that one will use to determine who you do business with for a transaction or on a regular basis. However, because many people are considering Klout Scores as a factor in deciding who to do business with, it is most important—particularly for thought leaders—to be aware of it and work to enhance it.

A few years ago, it was imperative that you had to know certain basics about a computer to get a job. This included how to turn it on (yes, that was a requirement that some didn't know!), how to use Lotus 1-2-3, WordPerfect (a popular predecessor of Microsoft Word), and a few other programs. Years later, you had to be knowledgeable about the Internet and how to do a Google search, how to send an e-mail, and other basic instructions. These were actual requirements to get a job.

Today, the focus has shifted to being social media savvy. Much of our world is centered around who has the most influence. So, if you're planning to survive in this new world, this new reality, this is a subject you only dismiss at your own career peril. So, hop on board and come with us as we continue to explore not only what makes for social media success but how you can make a direct link between the activities you do on social media and your Klout Score.

Klout is a very valuable tool for highlighting influential experts, and showing their areas of expertise. I use it as one of the filters when connecting with people I don't already know, to see if they really are walking their talk.[4]
**—ALAN STEVENS, SPEAKER, AUTHOR,
PR EXPERT, AND MEDIA COACH**

CHAPTER 3

Creating Content That Connects with Customers to Improve Your Klout Score

How can you squander even one more day not taking advantage of the greatest shifts of our generation? How dare you settle for less when the world has made it so easy for you to be remarkable?
—SETH GODIN, BESTSELLING AUTHOR

We have so much to do nowadays. If you are a thought leader and trying to get your message out to a very busy world, you know you don't have time to waste on trivial matters. Instead, each moment of your day has to be tightly focused on what has to be done to accomplish the tasks at hand.

Social media takes time to do it right. Oh sure, you could send out a bunch of information that is little more than a twenty-first-century version of a mimeographed newsletter, but that only hurts you in the long run. You want to be known as the person who sends out good information on a regular basis that is worth "paying for" in terms of time.

In writing this book, we interviewed the distinguished British journalist, author, and professional speaker Alan Stevens. Stevens is a seasoned communicator who has long understood the importance of influence. His weekly blog, Media Coach, deals with what is happening in the world of social media. He understands that a Klout Score is important and that engaging with one's community is imperative to being influential today.

In the interview we had with him for this book, Stevens said that the biggest mistake people make in social media is treating it like they are a broadcaster.[1] He stressed the importance of engaging in a dialog with others and making communication a two-way street. You can see the full version of the interview at http://KloutMatters.com/videos-and-more. You can also reach this site by scanning the following QR code with your smart phone.

Today much of what is on the net is offered for free. That is a good marketing tool and can help a dedicated marketer when implemented properly.

But we have to remember that "free" isn't necessarily "free." It costs you not necessarily in your wallet, but in the most expensive commodity you have—time! You want your content to matter more than ever, to be relevant to your market, and to be worth people's time.

This is what matters in social media, and it is what matters in your Klout Score. Your Klout Score is merely a reflection of the amount of influence you are exerting in the world in a given area. By creating content that is relevant and attractive to your customers, you increase your influence. When you have, for instance, a post that addresses a particular need that your customers have, they are willing to "pay" with their time giving you attention and reacting to your thoughts. In their reaction on social media, your Klout Score is raised.

What Joe Sugarman Taught Us

Joe Sugarman is a legendary marketer who has sold millions of dollars' worth of materials for his clients and his own companies. He is known as a legendary marketer who uses the power of psychology to get work done and increase sales.

He doesn't do this with some mystical, hypnotic power. Instead, Joe appeals to his clients by coming across as a "genuine, real guy" they can trust. Through years of consistent sharing and giving advice, Joe has built trust for his followers. He does his research to find out what problems his potential customers are facing, then blends those needs into his work so that customers are delighted to not only hear about what he has, but to buy it. What Joe Sugarman has done with marketing through the years is what thought leaders must do today— appeal to the audience by thinking from their point of view.

To raise your Klout Score, you will need to increase engagement from others for your work. As you see life from your audience's point of view, they will feel you are speaking to them and understand them. That is what true engagement in social media is all about. A Klout Score is merely a reflection of how much others react to what you are saying.

Good salespeople and marketers have known how to think like customers. In today's world of social media, the principles are the same. As you think like your audience thinks, you create content that they consider "must read" and they react to you. When they read, listen, and watch what you create, they will react in social media, and this helps to boost your Klout Score.

CHAPTER 4

Does Your Klout Score Really Matter?

While you may abhor the idea of a company like Klout judging or grading you on a daily basis, it's already happening and companies are paying attention, so we shouldn't just ignore this trend.
—MARK W. SCHAEFER, AUTHOR OF *THE TAO OF TWITTER*
AND *RETURN ON INFLUENCE*

Your Klout Score matters—a great deal. It matters in different ways for different people, depending on what line of work you do, who is making the decision, and how you will use your Klout Score.

Increasingly more decisions are being made on who to hire for full-time employment or for a specific contract across different industries. For instance, we know that many actors are being rejected or accepted by directors and producers for a part based on their Klout Scores. At the same time, people usually do not choose their auto repair shop to fix their car based on a Klout Score.

We see two aspects to the use of your Klout Score. One aspect is how the individual will use it to improve his or her performance. The other is how the rest of the world uses it to judge or evaluate that individual.

- **Self:** An individual should use the Klout Score much like you would use a bathroom scale to get your weight. Your Klout Score is a measurement of your social media effectiveness.
- **Others:** Your Klout Score is visible to the public, and consequently others may use it to judge you. This may include, but is not limited to, customers, business partners, media, investors, conference planners, competitors, brands, and others.

If you have a Twitter account, you have a Klout Score, which will be visible to the public, unless you follow Klout's procedure to make it invisible.

Your Klout Score matters differently depending on the type of business you have. Considerations include the size and scope of your business. Are you a global brand? Are you an individual who does business globally? Are you a local business that operates in a targeted geographical area?

Global Individual

The first type of business we are calling a global individual. This is what a thought leader really is. An example would be someone like Mari Smith, an expert on Facebook and a popular conference speaker and marketer. A thought leader is not limited to any specific geographical area; however, a thought leader often focuses on a given area of expertise. This can include speakers, authors, consultants, coaches, and others who share their thoughts and ideas with the world.

For this type of individual, a Klout Score matters a great deal. It matters as a gauge for one's own activity. In addition, it also matters to customers, business partners, media, investors, conference organizers, and other people who are making decisions regarding which thought leaders they are going to use. For example, a book publisher could use a potential author's Klout Score to determine how influential this person is—which could make a difference in selling books.

Local Business

In contrast to the individual thought leader, there is the local business. This is defined as someone who focuses his or her marketing on a given geographical area to provide products or services. Examples would include medical doctors, restaurants, salons, boutiques, and others. The case could be made that many customers are not selecting professionals in these categories based on a Klout Score currently. Yet business managers can look at their Klout Score as a directional beacon to determine the effectiveness of their own social media marketing. Following the principles that help to build your Klout Score will help you engage with customers and generate more business.

Another example of using a Klout Score would be for a local business to seek out key influencers. As an example, a restaurant might want to target those particular customers who have a high Klout Score. These individuals could be offered certain discounts or VIP treatment. These customers would then be able to talk about the service they received and the quality of food at the restaurant. For the restaurant owner, this could be one of the best ways to expand advertising and marketing dollars.

Klout Scores could be more important for local businesses in the future if Klout were to add a platform like Yelp, for example. Klout is continually examining many social media platforms to determine which would be appropriate to include as part of the Klout Score.

Global Brand

Let's take the case of a global brand. Most customers are not going to search for a car based on the Klout Score of the company. At first glance, it might seem that Klout Score does not matter to a global brand. It does matter as that brand examines what the marketplace is saying about it and its activity in social media. As we write this, Ford Motor Company, for instance, has a Klout Score of 92. Are people basing their purchases of Ford cars on the Klout Score? We don't think they are. However, this number is telling Ford Motor Company marketing executives that their engagement with social media is working.

From a bottom-line point of view, the logical question would be, "Does social media really matter in business?" Today the answer is an emphatic yes! According to Ragan's PR Daily news site:

A JD Power and Associates report finds that among those whose overall satisfaction with a company's social marketing efforts is "highly satisfied," 87 percent say their online social interaction with the company positively affected their likelihood to purchase from that company.

Basically, if a person likes the way you do social interactions, they're much more likely to buy your product. It's something we've suspected for some time and have the qualitative data to support, but this is one of the first studies that quantifies it.[1]

You want your content to matter more than ever, to be relevant to your market, and to be worth people's time. This is what matters in social media, and it is what matters in your Klout Score. Your Klout Score is merely a reflection of the amount of influence you are exerting in the world in a given area.

As we start to take ownership of our personal information, including original content and creative works via personal clouds, it is going to become more and more important to use social scoring as a means of verifying identity and reputation.
—KIMBERLY REYNOLDS, SOCIAL MEDIA AND MOBILE MARKETING STRATEGIST

CHAPTER 5

Should You Make an Effort to Increase Your Klout Score?

Everyone wants more impact, influence, branding, and recognition.
On the Internet it's known as Klout.
—JEFFREY GITOMER, BESTSELLING AUTHOR OF *THE LITTLE RED BOOK*
OF SELLING AND *21.5 UNBREAKABLE LAWS OF SELLING*

L et's face it, we are all pressed for time in today's hyper-busy environment. Any effort you expend in one area is going to take
away from effort you could have expended in another area. This is
what economists call your opportunity cost. It is something that every
thought leader and entrepreneur today has to consider regardless of
the task in which they are engaged.

Your Klout Score is a series of algorithms that have been devised to
determine the level of influence that a given individual has in any particular field. Because it is ultimately subjective, there will be some complaints about it, particularly from those who have lower Klout Scores.

Klout tells us that the average score is 40. Therefore if you have a
score of, say, 50, your score is above average. If your Klout Score is
significantly below 40, then you have a decision to make. If you were
trying to exert more influence in a particular area, then you might
want to perform those activities that help to enhance a Klout Score.
Creating compelling content is the most natural way to increase your
Klout Score and gain more influence among others.

You often hear people talk about the importance of creating compelling content. This is true and cannot be overstressed. We think

that the key word in that admonition is *compelling*. If you produce boring content, it is even worse than producing no content at all. The next question that arises is often, "How do you define *compelling content?*" This is a highly subjective term in that each thought leader can have a different definition. We like to describe it this way:

Compelling content is text, audio, video, pictures, or graphics that grab people's attention and make it worth their while to spend time consuming that. Compelling content will answer an important question, solve a problem, provide a solid benefit, be entertaining, or ultimately help the person consuming the content in business and/or his or her personal life. In the old days we would've called that a TV program or a magazine article. Today we call it content.

You have to invest time and effort into the process. Sometimes you'll invest money to come up with content that your audiences deem compelling. Compelling is more than merely interesting. It means that the person watching your video or reading your post values spending time to absorb your created material more than putting that time to use with other activities.

This is where successful people stand out from others. Many people will produce lots of content, but it is not worth reading for their target market. How do we know this? We know this because we can see the quantitative results of how few people actually read much content that is available on the net.

The whole realm of social experience and social media measurement is now becoming a strong factor in decision making. As cruel and mechanistic as it might sound, often people are selected based on a quantifiable score. This score is often one's Klout Score.

It's a different world than it was even a couple of years ago. There are more thought leaders all the time who are competing for attention. Attention has become one of the most valuable commodities that people have. In today's hotly competitive world, attention and time are two of the most valuable assets that anyone has.

Therefore every piece of content that you produce and distribute should be very compelling and well worth the time and attention that your readers, viewers, or listeners give you. We like the way that Craig

Duswalt says it when he recommends to "Always do your best, just in case someone is watching."[1]

We would have to agree with Craig in that yes, in the age of the Internet and long-lasting content, someone, somewhere, at some time may be reading, viewing, or listening to what you put on the net. Make sure that every piece of content you put on the net is in the excellent category. That should be your driving goal as a thought leader.

Social media strategist Kathryn Rose summed up what is most effective in social media very succinctly when she said: "Social media is not about spreading salesy messages, it's about growing a responsive community. Those with influence understand that it's all about relationships. It doesn't matter how many followers or friends, it's if they are responsive, engaged and communicative. It's about spreading useful, helpful content that will ultimately lead them to like, know, and trust you enough to pass it on. That is influence."[2]

It is also worth noting that once you get your Klout Score to a certain level, it becomes increasingly difficult to raise it further. For instance, if you have a Klout Score in the 70s, it becomes increasingly difficult to raise that merely by writing more compelling content. Writing the content alone is just the beginning. You need other people to talk about it and "amplify" what you were doing. If you write a blog, for instance, and several hundred thousand people tweet about that, then your Klout Score will inevitably increase. Conversely, if you write a great blog post enriched with compelling content, but no one recognizes it, your Klout Score will probably decline.

The key is in the combination. From a marketing point of view it is much like the old marketing story of having the best restaurant in the middle of nowhere where no one comes to dine with you. You can have the best food in the world, but if no one knows about it or comes to visit and dine with you, what's the point?

Klout will calculate your influence based on the number of tweets or messages that you send out on Twitter along with posts that you have on Facebook and other platforms. However, it doesn't stop there. What matters even more is not what you send out but how others respond to what you say and what action they take as a result of your posts. The number of retweets, @ mentions, and references by others you have on Twitter will make a difference in your Klout Score. Your goal as a content creator and thought leader is to create content that will make others want to acknowledge your work by retweeting it, reposting it, liking it, and other forms of acknowledgment. Let this drive your thinking as you begin the process of content creation.

As you produce professional, quality content on Facebook, you'll have a competitive advantage over others who don't produce top quality posts. On Facebook you have over 1 billion people who are generating content. Most of it is not professional, so you can have a slight competitive advantage when you produce material that is read by more people. Just producing free content in today's environment is not enough. It has to be something that people make an effort to find and read.

You have to be better in terms of professionalism that is tailored to your audience. You have to be consistent. You have to produce like a pro.

If you're looking for an easy answer on how to raise your Klout Score, this is most important. It is not as important what you put out into the world of social media. What is much more important is how others react to what you have done and the degree to which they take action. This action should be in the form of something that is tangible. Online that means that they can retweet what you do on Twitter or they can repost, comment, or like something you do on Facebook.

If you have a lot of retweets, then you are more influential than someone who doesn't get a lot of retweets. Remember, with Twitter, a tweet is the message you send out, and a retweet would be a message you posted and someone resends to his or her own followers.

Similar types of things can be said about Facebook. If you create a post on Facebook and a lot of people "like" it, then you have more influence. The more people who "like" or make comments on your post, the more your Klout Score will be affected in a positive way. Merely posting on Facebook is not sufficient.

The same can be said for other platforms where you have a presence. It is not enough to simply be there and to have a membership on a given platform. To use a real-life analogy, it would be like joining 15 Chambers of Commerce in your area and not being active in any. Just like in the real world, your Klout Score is going to be greatly affected by the level of participation that you have and that others have with you.

We like the way that Brian Tracy said it in his audio series *Getting Rich in America*: "Your success in life will largely be determined by the number of people who know you in a favorable way."[3] We can paraphrase Brian Tracy and move it into the realm of the Klout Score by saying "Your Klout Score will largely be determined by the number of people who interact with you and with whom you engage on a regular basis."

The people at Klout have taken great efforts to devise an algorithm and a system that measures the level of influence that people have. Is it perfect? Absolutely not! They will admit that themselves in the work that they have done. Joe Fernandez and his team at Klout let us know that their system is a work in progress. In a world that is constantly changing and morphing, this makes eminent business sense.

We look at it much as Nielsen would use television ratings to try to determine how many people are watching each program on television for a given night. Most reasonable people would believe that the scoring system is "close enough" to being accurate that we need to pay attention to it.

Our point throughout this book is that the elements that contribute to overall business success and marketing effectiveness are what you need to focus on to build your business—and subsequently enhance your Klout Score.

Remember our analogy of the BMI? If a patient weighs 500 pounds, smokes 14 packs of cigarettes a day, and drinks four quarts of Jack Daniels a day, that patient would objectively be in serious need of medical help. The patient would not be motivated to go to the doctor only to get a better BMI score. The patient would need to work closely with a medical care professional to drop the weight, eliminate negative habits, and increase positive health-giving habits over a reasonable period of time.

This is our premise about the Klout Score. If thought leaders engage in the proper marketing activity to involve themselves with their target market, they will naturally generate more business. As more business is generated, they will become more influential, resulting in a higher Klout Score.

It will take a commitment to devoting your resources of time, money, and effort to be successful with social media and the world of Klout. Kim Garst, social media speaker and cofounder of Boom! Social, put it very succinctly:

Social media isn't FREE!

*One of the biggest hurdles for a small business to real-
ize is that while social media accounts do not take money to
get started, the management of social media marketing is a
profession. Like a profession, it takes the investment of time,
knowledge, and effort. It takes time and effort to create a truly
engaging and effective brand presence, and this takes a financial commitment, just like any other form of marketing activity. Adding social media duties to the workloads of people
who are not trained in effectively engaging with an audience
is ineffective at best and could be horrendous at worst. (Have
you heard any of the Twitter stories out there where someone
tweeted something rude or inappropriate on a brand's Twitter
account?)*[4]

Kim Garst told us even more about how you can build your
community and what it takes to succeed in social media.[5] This is
described in more detail in the video that accompanies this book,
which you can view at http://KloutMatters.com/videos-and-more.
You can also reach this site by scanning the QR code below with
your smartphone.

While it does require a commitment of time, money, and effort to
make social media work for you, it is something that should be fun.
If it is not fun, you need to either figure out a way to make it fun
or change fields! Edel O'Mahoney, a UK-based speaker and active
social media user, put it well when she said, "Stop looking on social
media as a chore! Social media is essential in the digital age of global
communications. Look on your social media as expanding your conversation with the world. When it becomes communication through
conversation, it is seen and valued as personal."[6]

So the proper way for a busy thought leader to engage in social media would be to focus on those key areas that help to enhance and build one's business regardless if a Klout Score exists or not. Pretend that Klout had never been developed. The principles that we're talking about in this book work not only in social media but also with business in general. It is most important to engage with customers and clients wherever and however you operate.

The system of assigning a score to your digital influence is really a tracking point to make sure you are doing the right activities. Like the analogy we suggested in the Introduction, think of Klout as the lighthouse, off in the distance, that is guiding your small rowboat through a storm-ravaged sea. Klout provides a set of activities with which you can engage to achieve business success—and also raise your Klout Score!

Entrepreneur magazine had an article about how Justin Bieber is creating a lot of attention. He is known for having a score of 100 at one time (before a Klout system-wide revision). Even though he is known as a singer with a following largely of teenage girls, he is practicing some very sound business principles. Among these are: (1) have real conversations with followers, (2) get retweeted often, and (3) tweet for charity. All of these points help to build credibility and authority, and they boost your Klout Score when done in an authentic, genuine way.[7]

In this work, we will show you some specific techniques that can help you develop your Klout Score on specific platforms like Twitter, Facebook, and others. Some might call this gaming the system. In our next chapter we plan to look specifically at the idea of gaming the system and what it means and what not to do.

CHAPTER 6

What About Gaming the System?

Your emphasis must be on consistently creating compelling content. You can't game the system simply by promoting a lot of other people who were all promoting another person. The idea of several people simply promoting each other reminds me of the link farms that we saw before where many people ask to link to the other simply because they wanted to link to them and it ended up with a link farm. Google would quickly sandbox these people.

This is similar to trying to boost your Google page rank. You have to produce compelling content first. Then you work with others who can help you and promote you. And yes, reciprocity kicks in because you help them as they help you. Even more important, if you begin by promoting and helping others, they in turn will want to help you where they can.

Some might contend that using certain techniques and tricks are just gaming the system and don't really "count." Well, that is a nice knee-jerk reaction, and it is important enough to merit careful consideration.

Aaron Lee has a blog that addresses many relevant issues for marketers. A while back he had a post about Klout and techniques that can be used to boost a Klout Score.[1] In that post he mentioned doing certain activities such as niche tweets, quotes from your niche, and photos. One could argue that these are mere gaming strategies for boosting one's Klout Score.

We would disagree. What Aaron is submitting in this particular post makes a lot of sense. One can call it gaming, but we contend it is doing sound marketing in a unique way.

For instance, marketing to a niche is a sound principle for building your base. We think of the quote from Bill Cosby, who said, "I don't know what it takes to be successful, but I do know that the key to failure is trying to please everyone." This principle applies to your work with social media and your Klout Score. Your best results come from focusing on a particular area of expertise and building your audience and fan base there. Don't try to be all things to everyone in social media. That strategy doesn't work in real life, and it won't work in the online social media world. Those who do best are those who focus and stop trying to please everyone. Have an opinion on a hot topic, express it eloquently and in an entertaining way, and you'll build your audience. In building that audience, you'll be able to enhance your Klout Score. What Aaron Lee talks about in this post makes sound sense whether Klout exists or not.

The idea of using photos makes a lot of sense because we learned that long ago. The creators of the Sears Roebuck catalog (when it was known by that name) learned early on that pictures were very important in selling merchandise. Was Sears Roebuck gaming the system? We think Sears was simply deploying sound marketing and psychological principles and tactics that worked to sell more merchandise.

There are many tactics that others will use that are based on sound marketing principles that work over time to generate more business. This is where we need to concentrate our efforts.

The problems of "gaming" are those techniques that are not sustainable. These measures don't rely on sound business practices or what will work long term in marketing. Tricks like getting several people to all "like" each other's page can provide a short-term boost in a Klout Score. This is much like a "birthday boost" where your Klout Score can jump as many people wish you a happy birthday. However, the rise in your Klout Score diminishes after the birthday wishes are over. Those who try to get a group of people to artificially "like" each other's pages for no specific reason generate only a temporary bump in their Klout Score.

These methods are what our friend Mark Schaefer refers to as "icky." We have to admit that we love Mark's eloquence and way of describing this so adroitly! What would be some of the "icky" ways of gaming the system? The following are "icky" tactics we recommend you avoid.

"Like" Farms

The term *"like" farm* is one that we borrow from an earlier time of link farms. It used to be that many websites would try to get other websites to link to them. This was a good practice as people who have similar websites could promote other like-minded websites for the betterment of content creation.

However, the challenge here was that many people linked to sites that had no reference whatsoever to their own site. They simply were gaming the system to try to beat the search engine optimization (SEO) rankings that Google assigned.

Those conducting this practice hardly knew or had hardly any relationship to what was being advanced on the linked websites. They just wanted to have links. The idea was that Google would give you a higher SEO ranking if you had many links.

Well, these didn't last very long as Google saw what was happening and immediately banned sites that were engaged in such link farms. In fact, Google was known to "sandbox" many of these sites. Being "sandboxed" meant that you lost a ranking and had severe damage in the search engine optimization war. Google would sometimes lower the ranking of a site or ban it outright from its ranking system.

Years ago, and now as well, it was not just a matter of how many links you had from others. Instead it mattered where those links came from and whether the links came from sites that had a high number of visitors. For instance, you will have a better Google rank if you have links from many popular sites like CNN.com, Foxnews.com, MSNBC.com, CNBC.com, the *New York Times*, and other high-value websites. The same is true in the social media world. You get a higher Klout Score if those who are influenced by you have very high Klout Scores. If you get a bunch of likes and mentions from people like Justin Bieber, Barack Obama, Oprah Winfrey, and Ellen DeGeneres (all of whom have Klout Scores in the 90s as of this writing), you are going to also have a higher Klout Score.

Today, Klout is known to watch out for any Klout gaming that might be attempted. Klout can override the automatic calculation of a Klout Score and downgrade it when it detects that users are engaging in certain disreputable activities.

So step back and think about it. If you are a thought leader, where should you invest your activity? You can try to get a higher Klout Score by linking to someone and artificially punching up your Klout Score for a day or two, but that ultimately doesn't last.

What does last, and is based on sound marketing practices, is to engage with customers, provide content that is compelling, and sustain that over a period of time. It is really that simple—but this is not easy.

We've seen examples of groups that will have a number of group members commit to helping each other promote a given post over a day. That is fine, as far as it goes. It is often common for a person to help promote a special sale that someone might have for a given item or a book, for instance. Many people will try to boost the sale of a book on a given day when it launches so that it can reach a *New York Times* bestseller status. However, if the book soars to the top of the charts on one day and then falls into oblivion shortly thereafter, this is a pointless feat. Any true success must be sustainable. The ideal is that you have a product that grows over time and maintains a status of providing quality to a large number of growing fans and users.

Trying to game the system is only temporarily helpful, whether it's using Klout or in any other area. Many times people try to game the system of Nielsen or Arbitron television and radio ratings. That might boost the ratings of a television or radio station for one short period of time, but in the long term it will not work.

If you are a professional speaker, a coach, an author, a blogger, or another form of thought leader, you need to create compelling content on a sustainable basis. Merely trying to use some trick of the moment to get your Klout Score advanced is not going to work.

If you are trying to boost your Klout Score only to get a particular job, gaming the system is not the strategy to employ. For your employer to be pleased with having you on board, its leaders will need to see a sustained higher level of achievement. This means that you have to meet the needs of clients by producing quality content and promoting it accordingly.

Like many things in life, there is a balance to be achieved here. You do not want to game the system. However, working in collaboration with others can pay rich dividends. In Chapter 16 we talk about the importance of online collaborative networks. If you have an agreement with a carefully selected group of people to help each other promote, it can help you in business as well as your Klout Score.

Buying Twitter Followers

Here's a gaming strategy that some have tried in the past. Many people will try to hire false followers in Twitter to boost their Klout Score. This is silly and a waste of your money because the total number of followers has very little impact on your Klout Score. What matters much more is the number of people with whom you *engage* (there's that word again!).

Some people mistakenly think that by adding more followers they will be able to exert more influence. This is both shortsighted and expensive. You want to have real people who were acquired through genuine contact in social media. One of the best ways to achieve this is for them to hear your presentations. If you are a professional speaker, you'll want many people to hear you and for those people to admire you so much and love your content so much that they want to stay in touch with you.

What really contributes to a Klout Score is the degree to which people interact with you and your content and then pass it along with their recommendation to others. You want to concentrate on creating profound, compelling content that people listen to and then pass to their followers, who in turn pass it along to their followers, and so on—you get the idea. This is really the essence of viral marketing. You want many people to pass along your content so that it grows naturally, without a lot of force and hype, but this only happens when you have solid content that is profound and powerful on a consistent basis. In other words, you've got to be good! If you're not there yet, keep practicing and get better all the time. That is a key to engaging more with customers, boosting your digital influence—and raising your Klout Score for success!

This is the same concept that worked back in the 1800s when Fyodor Dostoyevsky wrote his great novels. Dostoyevsky created great novels that people wanted to share with others, so they bought them and encouraged others to buy them as well. It took time, yet his novels still remain classics today—and no, Fyodor Dostoyevsky never engaged in any Klout link farms that we know about!

Acquiring people who are genuinely interested in you and raise their hand saying, "Yes, I want to follow her" is a valid marketing strategy. This is the best way for true thought leaders to build their influence.

Doing the +K Gig

Here's a clever approach that is based on helping but can end up causing problems. Klout will give extra bonus points toward your Klout Score if a number of other Klout users give you what's called a +K. This is a nice way of saying yes, this person has influence in a given area. It can be a good thing that a number of people recognize you have expertise in, say, writing. You may say that you are a good writer, but if many other people are saying you're a good writer as well, this will serve as proof of your talent. And their opinion will carry a lot more weight.

However, the challenge comes when many people try to simply give each other +Ks over and over, and you get the same people giving the same people +Ks every day. That tends to make the compliments rather hollow in their genuineness.

It is always good to compliment another in a genuine way. Think about being at the local Chamber of Commerce in the 1940s when someone might stand up and say, "Thank you, Bob, for the great work you did on building the dam to save us from the raging rivers." This hypothetical compliment to Bob in the 1940s would be nice and would engender good feelings toward Bob by all those present at the 1940s Chamber of Commerce meeting. It would be a 1940s version of a +K.

However, to continue this 1940s example, if every week you stood up and thanked Bob for saving the village with the dam, the effect would soon be lost.

Our point is that a +K is a genuine way to say hello to people and to help them, but don't do it with the same people over and over. Make sure that you use it in a sincere way and for a number of different people.

If you were able to reach a lot of different people and give them genuine benefits, then that is good. This is what business is all about—complementing others and helping them to achieve the goals they want.

Kare Anderson is a columnist with the Huffington Post and *Forbes* magazine. In a video we did with her for this book, she said that social media is really about "shining a bright light on what you most admire in others."[2] This type of genuine praise, not insincere flattery, helps to build your community and enhance your digital influence. You can see the video interview we had with Kare at http://KloutMatters.com/videos-and-more. You can also reach this site by scanning the following QR code with your smartphone.

Using the ability to give +Ks to your friends is nice; however, this should not be your focus. Think of it like waving hello to someone on the other side of a noisy, busy restaurant. It is nice, but you can't build a solid relationship on that alone. If, however, that "wave across the restaurant" leads to you getting up and walking over to talk with someone, that's a different story! Remember that real, genuine engagement with customers and others is the key to success in social media.

It is genuine, real engagement that matters most with Klout and bottom-line results.

Long-Term Damage to Your Reputation

This is probably the most serious problem. There are many ways that people will try to game the system in Klout. This is natural because people try to game the system in whatever is a popular tool of the day. The challenge comes long after it is "cool" to use that particular tool and your reputation still remains tarnished.

As an example, Terry once knew a person on the West Coast who was constantly involved in various multilevel marketing programs.

There's nothing wrong with multilevel marketing. We think it is a very good way for people to earn a living and to help other people when it is done right.

However, when many of us would think of this particular individual, we realized that every time we talked to him, he was always onto a new gig. Nothing seemed to last much longer than a few months, and his reputation for any kind of sustainable marketing growth in business never materialized. Whenever you would talk to him, he was excited about the new deal of the moment. However, after you got to know him for a while, you realized that the new deal of the moment would be replaced with a newer deal of the moment a few weeks later.

When someone becomes known as the "multilevel guy," it becomes a problem. When your reputation becomes tied to whatever the cool nifty gadget of the moment is, you suffer long-term damage. You develop a reputation as someone who is not reliable, and who relies on only the latest trend of the moment.

"Gaming the system" is not a reliable way to create sustainable marketing business growth or a good reputation. Yes, these techniques can work for a short time, and they might give you a momentary boost in your Klout Score. But remember that any sustained, long-term, useful, reliable, and credible marketing is done through certain practices that have worked throughout time.

You want to focus your efforts on those tried and true practices that demonstrate marketing credibility over time. Focus on what matters most rather than the shiny new object of the day.

This is sustainable over the long term, not just for a quick fix. It is often a good rule of thumb in life to avoid the quick fix and to focus on what is going to be a long-term benefit for you and for those around you. This same principle applies to your Klout Score.

In a marketplace that is changing fast, techniques and tactics can change rapidly. The good news is that time-honored principles stand and will always work. Spend your time, money, and effort learning and applying the principles of connecting and engaging with buyers—whatever the technology of the moment happens to be.

Some of you may have purchased this book to find out new gaming strategies that can help lead to higher Klout Scores. If you are one of those people, we welcome you aboard and look forward to seeing great content that you will create and great business practices that you will implement to help people stay with you.

Use this as your filter for the future: don't focus on the latest technique or technology to build your business. Focus your time, money, and effort on genuinely increasing value in the marketplace through content and contributing to the value creation of others.

When you think about it, building your Klout Score comes from practicing sound business policies. This is important no matter what the technology of the day is. Terry has written extensively in his earlier work and in his blog about relationship marketing. He says that success in business is not about e-commerce (electronics); it is about r-commerce (relationships).

True business success comes from doing those activities that your mama probably told you were important:

- Listen to others.
- Care about what matters to them.
- Provide lots of value (think content with blog, audio, and video creation).
- Engage with customers.
- Genuinely provide help.
- Help others generate business.

All of these principles are important, and as you practice them, you will be able to build your business on a sustainable, long-term basis. Focus on these proven and reliable activities and you will not regret it.

CHAPTER 7

The Role of Vendors and Perks

Fame can be annoying, but there are perks too.
—DANICA PATRICK

Social media is changing the way manufacturers reach consumers. In the past, a manufacturer would simply blanket a market by buying a lot of radio, television, newspaper, and other forms of advertising. Today it is better to focus on key influencers and have them talking about your product or service rather than the other way around.

As an example, Sandy Weaver Carmen is a friend of ours who has a distinguished background in radio and voice-over talent. Sandy's offline passion is her love of dogs, specifically the Siberian huskies that she owns. Sandy is a judge at many dog contests and travels around the country judging dogs, including Siberian huskies. When Sandy makes a recommendation about dog food, for instance, many people will pay attention to what she has to say.

A company like Flint River Ranch, which makes dog food, would be very wise to focus on someone like Sandy who is very influential with the buyers of their products. In the past, advertisers who wanted to reach a given market would pay a lot of money to the local TV and radio stations along with newspapers, perhaps some outdoor advertising, and other promotional media to get attention.

Today their money could be much better spent by focusing on a person like Sandy and giving her the information she needs to evaluate their products. Then they can let Sandy recommend their products to her market. Imagine that if instead of spending all your limited advertising dollars on mass media, you could target those key people who are most influential in areas where your buyers congregate.

Engaging your target market with highly influential people (an army of "Sandys," if you will) is often a much better use of your limited dollars and results in much more sales. This is another example of what we call "advocate marketing."

Throughout history, makers of everything from carefully crafted ancient bazaar rugs to ultramodern high-tech equipment have wanted to sell through the right people. They knew that reaching influencers and having those key influencers say nice things about their products meant that more people would pay attention.

That is the revolution of social media. Today, the marketplace has been turned upside down. Instead of advertisers calling all the shots, the consumers control what has credibility. The more influential the consumers who are saying good or bad things about a given product or service, the more the message will be magnified.

This is the essence of what is happening with Klout. But many people have objected to Klout being seen as the "be all and end all" of measuring influence in today's world.

Criticisms of Klout

Klout is not based on the realization that there are many areas of influence it just doesn't—and probably can't—measure adequately. However, that doesn't mean Klout doesn't address important concerns about who is more influential than others in certain areas.

It only makes sense that in a world that is becoming increasingly concerned with quantitative methods, we are going to want to measure people's influence by a certain scale. We secretly think that we are all looking for the way to measure ourselves against others and hope that we have a higher score than our competitors—or even our friends. However, when our own score is lower than our friends' scores, we object to the system.

Klout has not been without its detractors. From the beginning many have questioned the use of any type of metric to measure one's influence. There are many who contend that trying to assign a numerical figure to something as squishy and highly subjective as influence is as ludicrous as trying to grasp quicksilver.

As with many controversies in life, we have to take it with a grain of salt.

We think this is an argument that has some merit, but the detractors often go too far. It is very much like we're playing elementary school all over again with the "cool kids" versus the "others." If people receive a high Klout Score, they feel the system is fine and are glad to be ranked so well. If their Klout Score is lower, or if it is degraded by a recent revision of the scoring system, they go into outrage.

John Scalzi is the author of one of the oldest blogs, entitled *Whatever*. It is a very insightful blog and has done good work in promoting some noteworthy causes. Scalzi wrote a post on CNNMoney entitled "Why Klout Scores Are Possibly Evil" that raised some eyebrows in the online world. In that post, Scalzi made a point when he said:

> *Who made Klout the arbiter of online influence, aside from Klout itself? I could rank your influence online. If you like: I'll add your number of Twitter followers to your number of Facebook friends, subtract the number of MySpace friends, laugh and point if you're still on Friendster, take the square root, round up to the nearest integer, and add six. That's your Scalzi Number (mine is 172). You're welcome. Is this number any less indicative of your actual online popularity than Klout's scores? As far as you know, no.*[1]

There are many who boldly question why Klout can come up with an arbitrary number for people and have it hold any legitimacy. This is a worthy question when any organization contends to speak as the voice of authority to rank people. Going back to our high school analogy, it would be like the high school newspaper ranking all the kids in a class by their popularity.

People will ask, "Who gives them the right to rank each of us? What tools are they using to rank us and cast spurious doubts about who is more influential?"

These are good points, but they miss the bigger picture and issue. Klout exists. It has weight. It has more weight than all of its current competitors combined. If you look at tools like Kred, PowerIndex,

Appinions, and others competing to assess and assign influence, Klout is by far the leader today.

It is time to move beyond the arguments that were bandied about a few years ago. Klout is a presence that is considered by many to have authority and weight. Like it or not, it is a force we have to deal with in today's world. More important, our world is growing increasingly dependent on a quantitative analysis of what is happening in the marketplace. If you are a thought leader, you are going to be judged by many in many different ways. It is already important that many people consider your Klout Score. Even more important is that these people are buyers who make decisions on who to hire for various projects.

Recently Klout entered into an agreement with Microsoft's Bing search engine. It makes sense that if someone is searched on more often, then that person has more influence. For Bing, Klout is the vehicle it is using to include social endorsements in its search algorithm, similar to the way Google is using Google+ data.

Search engine/social scoring integration is still in its infancy. As such, there are a lot of details to work out. For example, one of Klout's challenges is that it is hard to figure out who you're talking about when many people have the same name.

An example close to home for us: we have discovered that there are many people named Terry Brock on the Internet. We know of at least one famous rock singer (formerly with the band Kansas), an archaeologist who attended Michigan State University, and a realtor in California, all of whom are named Terry Brock. There is even a famous tap dancer named Terry Brock—who is a woman! So how do you tell which Terry Brock is the Terry Brock writing this book?

In an effort to solve this problem and train Klout's system to recognize your name in context, Klout is asking users to connect their Klout account to Bing and to tag articles that are related to them.

Many thought leaders are now embracing the fact that people's Klout Score is being used to make buying decisions. They are definitely not obsessing over their Klout Score, but are paying attention to it. Those who are operating as the best social media citizens are those who engage in the right practices online (like those suggested in this book). As they engage in those practices in the right way, they have a natural, organic result of a higher Klout Score.

The relationship with Bing is highly significant. Microsoft wants to outshine Google and its search preference in the market. Bing is embracing social influence searching so that people can reference influence based on factors like the number of times a person or topic has been searched.

This is a relationship wise thought leaders will want to study and be aware of as it develops. Like many other features in digital media, this is the beginning of what can have significant impact on how decisions are made in digital influence.

We talk about this often between us and when we make presentations at various seminars and conferences. What is the proper balance between ignoring one's Klout Score completely and going to the other extreme and obsessing with the daily change? There are those who feel dejected and have a bad day if their Klout Score is decreased by a mere fraction of a few points. They are elated if it goes up even a few points.

Some people believe they can game the system and boost their Klout Score, thereby decreasing the validity of such a score. While there might be some things that can be done that boost engagement in the short run, these activities could include engaging in methods we expressed earlier such as "like" farms, trying to use a service to have robots like your pages on Facebook, and more. Klout's scoring algorithm is "smart" in that it learns about these things and corrects for them. Also, since the scoring considers a full 90 days of activity—with greater weighting of recent activity—it is hard to game the system for such an extended period that it would produce long-term scoring gains.

Nevertheless, the mere fact that someone can use clever adjustments to change their score does raise eyebrows about the entire validity of a scoring system for influence. The point could be made that if one can do certain tricks and adjust a Klout Score, then what's the point of caring about it at all? If one can engage in certain activities for a short period of time and get an artificial boost to a Klout Score, doesn't that decrease and diminish its relevance?

We understand this and have to agree with some of the basic concerns. Yes, there are certain techniques that can be used from time to time that can artificially boost a Klout Score for a short period of time. It would be very easy to use this "evidence" to dismiss any relevance whatsoever with a measuring system like Klout.

In the blog The Digital Drew, we read that your Klout Score could result in the death of the résumé and become a measurable currency.[2] Employers will look to hire people based on their Klout Score. Already it is known to be a factor when considering various candidates in a hotly contested marketplace.

This poses a serious concern, both for job candidates and for thought leaders looking to be hired. What realistic importance should one place on a Klout Score? Does this mean more than the experience you had or the educational background you had? Should an employer consider a candidate's current Klout Score more than his or her educational background? Without going to either extreme, what is the best approach for a professional to take today in this hyper-competitive marketplace?

The answer, as with so many concerns in life, is a healthy balance. Most of us have found that going to extremes on almost any issue is usually dangerous. To completely ignore your Klout Score is the ostrich approach. You can't "stick your head in the sand" and get by if you expect to be a credible thought leader in today's world.

At the same time, you're wasting valuable time, money, and effort if you continually obsess about your Klout Score. Those who engage in frivolous gaming of the system tactics wind up with only a short-term boost in their score.

The real key, of course, is to focus on doing those activities where you engage with customers and you build credibility that is sustainable over the long term. Regardless of the technology of the moment, it is important to provide content that people want to consume that solves a real-world problem. This is something that the amazing Chris Brogan, a well-known star in the world of social media, has been saying for years. We have to agree passionately with him about this. Social media is about connecting with people, and, for those of us making a living on it, paying attention to the bottom line. Chris talks about building his e-mail list and getting more customers as a focus. Once again, we agree completely with Mr. Brogan on this!

After content creation comes promotion, which is equally or more important. You might have written the greatest book on a very important topic, but if no one knows about it and there's no promotion, then you might as well not have written it.

In summary, the critics have some valid points. Yes, it is very difficult to get a true picture of how much influence someone has by measuring a set of algorithms. Yes, it is true that algorithms can be manipulated by certain temporary tricks. And yes, what matters most is not some temporary number that is given to you on a daily basis but a more composite picture of attributes, characteristics, background, and experience that contributes to influence.

Influence, like quicksilver, is hard to grab hold of and hang onto. Maintaining influence is a never-ending activity for thought leaders. Much like entertainers who are popular for a moment, then fall into oblivion, thought leaders need to continually create fresh ideas and content to remain relevant.

Scott Levy, writing for Forbes.com, recently posted an article about both Klout and Kred, the top competitor of Klout in the influence-marketing space. In that post, he complains about both products:

> *There was no transparency as to how they were coming up with these scores and what mattered. Yet some HR wannabe early adopters with no sense or ability to understand or make their own determinations about social media prowess actually made hiring decisions based on these scores—unbelievable, I know. As most people know, this score goes up and down daily and often without reason. In addition it's always been easily manipulated. Hire someone to spam your twitter handle (like some gurus I know) and all of the sudden you're a social rocket scientist. Apparently a 14-year-old screaming about Bieber every day is just as influential as an intelligent thought-provoking tech journalist with a solid following and engagement.[3]*

These criticisms come because some might think that a Klout Score is the only tool used in the hiring procedure. In addition to that, Levy's assertion about Justin Bieber fans being more influential than a thought-provoking tech journalist misses the point. Influence is best determined through topics of expertise.

Levy, and others who use arguments as he did, are correct that using a Klout Score alone to make a decision is usually not only wrong, but can lead to problems. It is best to factor a Klout Score into the decision-making mix when dealing with influencers.

Mark Fidelman is a *Forbes* columnist, author of the book *Socialized!*, and CEO of Evolve, a company in the influencer engagement marketplace. In a video interview we did for this book, Mark said that Klout is a great tool, but not perfect. He favors a balanced approach to measuring one's influence that can be derived from several sources.[4] Klout is a key component in determining one's influence, particularly with emphasis on the online involvement. You can see the complete video interview at http://KloutMatters.com/videos-and-more. You can also reach this site by scanning the following QR code with your smartphone.

In an interview with Joe Fernandez, cofounder and CEO of Klout, he said:

> *When you talk about it, people get caught up in the "that's a dangerous way to hire people." However, people don't give hiring managers the benefit of the doubt to use good judgment to do more than one factor. In today's market, a person's ability to leverage social media is a critical job factor for most positions. Ten years ago it was being comfortable on a PC, five years ago, being comfortable on the Internet. Now it is being comfortable on social media. Klout is the standard to measure that.[5]*

We understand and appreciate many of the criticisms of Klout. Joe acknowledges that Klout's scientists are human, not perfect, and they have made mistakes. Yet, Klout employees are not just a group of really smart, hardworking people. We see passion and a genuine, caring environment where the "Kloutlaws" (what they call employees of Klout) want to help people use social media tools in the best way possible so that each person is successful in what he or she needs. Klout often says that everyone is an influencer. Klout is out to help influencers perform best, based on proven analytics and data-driven results.

It is a work in progress, and we are at the early stages of it now. Joe Fernandez shared an idea with us as we sat talking with him at Klout headquarters. He said, "Think about where Google was in 1999. They were the best search engine then. However, they are much better now and have expanded into many other areas including maps, hardware, video, and more."[6]

Where we are today, with social influence measurement, is in the embryonic stages of this powerful tool called big data. It is normal that all players in this space will make mistakes. However, as we move forward with the right intentions, pure motives, and a genuine desire to help both consumers and brands, we will see some great benefits.

Those benefits include perks and brand involvement like never before.

Klout, Perks, and Brand Involvement

All of the scoring that is part of Klout is good, but a central question that will be asked is, "How is Klout going to make any money?"

Brands are looking to connect with key influencers. Klout has the data on who is influential. Klout can help brands to connect with key influencers so they can promote a given brand to their communities. The brands will be financially involved with Klout to get access to these influencers.

Klout makes a strong point that it will not release the confidential information of Klout users to the brands. No contact information transfer will take place from Klout to the brands about this. This helps to maintain a position of privacy.

The brands will make perks consisting of gifts, samples of the product, or a special treat. For instance, Chevy Volt can target consumers who are interested in cars and environmental issues by loaning them a car for a weekend. Virgin America gave free trips to some key influencers in the travel industry so they could be exposed to the service the airline offers.

Another way that Klout will make money is by providing data to companies like Genesys, which integrates Klout Scores into its customer service platform. Genesys integrates Klout Scores into the call center so it can better identify customers when they call for assistance. Those with high Klout Scores are recognized as such and may receive an advanced level of help and support.[7]

Klout also has a firm policy that influencers are not obligated to say positive things about the brand that gives them perks. This way the reviews can be more objective and therefore believable.

A smart brand can use some reverse engineering and careful observations to find out who is saying something about the brand. Tools like Hootsuite can track references to a product or brand. Of course, Google and Bing are devoted to doing this kind of search. More tools are on the horizon for monitoring this type of activity. Check to see what is current now with a Google search.

This is the real power of Klout. It is accumulating massive amounts of data on a regular basis. Over 12 billion points of contact are evaluated and measured daily to determine Klout Scores. Once that information is accumulated over time, a score is given to influencers.

For the influencers and users of Klout, that might seem like the end of the game (at least until tomorrow's score is revealed!). However, that's where the fun begins for the brands.

Brands then will be able to craft their marketing to work with key influencers so they engage in what we call advocate marketing. The brand is not promoting or touting its own product. Brands are letting highly influential people talk about their preferences, likes, dislikes, and more. Is this risky? Of course it is. However, that is where our world is today.

Randy Gage is the author of the *New York Times* bestseller *Risky Is the New Safe*. In that work he discusses how the world is different today. What used to be safe—a 40-year career with one company, followed by secure retirement and a gold watch—doesn't exist for most today. Taking risks is the best way to ensure your prosperity for the future.

So brands are taking that risk by being authentic and genuine with users. Those who successfully engage with users—and particularly with highly influential people—will do just fine.

All these considerations are important as Klout works with brands to determine how they can reach key influencers. With the right amount of targeting, brands can save a lot on their advertising expenditures. Targeting the right people is what effective advertising is all about.

At a recent South by Southwest (SXSW) event, Cirque du Soleil held an event and invited Klout users to register for special seating and treatment. They knew that by targeting those with a specific Klout Score and above they would attract attendees who are social media and tech savvy. They also counted on these people to talk about the event and help with the Cirque du Soleil message.[8]

As we were beginning our research for this book, we received a special gift. That gift was a conversation with someone we admire personally and professionally, Mark W. Schaefer. Mark is the author of *Return on Influence: The Revolutionary Power of Klout, Social Scoring, and Influence Marketing.* If you haven't read his book yet, you should do so as it contains a lot of great information.

Mark talked extensively about this area of brands and what needs to be done. We believe he summed up much of what social media is doing for brands and their relationships with consumers when he said to us, "The opportunity of social media is to allow brands and companies to build personal relationships through a series of small interactions."[9]

Brands are moving to involve themselves with customers more than ever. In the past they used the "spray and pray" marketing method of broadcasting a message to a mass of people hoping that somehow, someway, some of the people might come and buy the product.

Today, brands are connecting not only with customers, but with key influencers who can make decisions and, in turn, influence others. The advocate marketing approach is more precisely targeted at the right people and can generally be more cost-effective. Because the relationships between brands and consumers can become stronger over time, they are much deeper than a traditional quick transaction.

When we interviewed Jon Dick, manager of business development at Klout, he said that Klout is connecting with other partners to help them and Klout users. Jon talked about how bloggers were influential years ago (and still are today!) because they have a specific influence and knowledge in a given area. He said they are more like journalists who develop a loyal following over time.[10] This is where Klout is focusing on a new, more genuine and personal form of connecting brands with customers. The old "spray and pray" form of marketing is being replaced with a much more targeted, personal means of connecting.

Debbie Horovitch is a Toronto-based "social media concierge" who has had experience as a media buyer. Her insights on Klout are interesting as to where we are today:

> As a traditional media buyer for agencies for many years, we always priced/valued the ad space we'd buy based on the size and relative engagement of the audience. In Canada, we still rely on PMB, Print Measurement Bureau, to cross tabulate media consumption & brand purchases with our own determined segments of the population based on demographics & psychographics. But PMB is 20,000 interviews in-person per year, with a rolling 2-year results—so we can only see what's happening reliably as recently as 18 months on average. Klout is a really new media measurement platform, that gives instantaneous results, and I think it's incredibly valuable and will become an even more reliable tool for media buyers at ad agencies to determine active and engaged segments of the target groups where they should apply a portion of their annual media budgets to Klout Perks campaigns. Sadly, very few of the media buyers in my community even know what Klout is, and many of the PR/bloggers only use it to rank each other's egos.[11]

Perks are a fascinating topic regarding Klout. To cite a personal, and even humorous, example, Terry recently received a perk from Klout. The brand sending it was Axe hair gel. We're sure that Axe hair gel is very good for many people. However, if you've seen a picture of Terry recently, you know that with his shaved-head look, he doesn't have a need for a lot of hair gel! Terry accepted the offer partly because he was curious about it and even more so because he had no idea what hair gel was!

The most effective marketing really comes from knowing your customer and the needs and wants of that customer. The system is not perfect yet, but it is getting better. In a noisy system where there is a lot of clutter in advertising, it makes sense to use targeted gifts and perks toward those who are in a select market and meet select criteria.

A big factor in today's world is what is happening with mobile marketing. Smartphones provide the ability to connect with the world, get answers to just about any question, and do even more than we could with the most sophisticated laptop computer of 10 years ago.

Mobile will play a big part in the field of social influence. For instance, if you are traveling through a town you're visiting and want to know where to find a good sushi dinner, the combination of mobile and Klout can help. You can find the type of sushi restaurant that has been rated highly by those you respect. Various retail shops and restaurants would want to connect with people who have a higher Klout Score through mobile apps. The reason would be that these people are more likely to talk about the great service or products they get. We believe that mobile integrated with Klout Scores has strong benefits ahead for retailers and consumers.

The apps could suggest certain restaurants or other choices based on the data that a user has submitted. The opt-in system is the only one that will last or be accepted by people. You have to make sure the brand has been given permission to enter the user's world.

This is another step toward what Seth Godin calls permission-based marketing. This is better for brands in that they will save money by spending their limited budgets on those people who are most likely to buy their products rather than using "spray and pray" marketing. This is better for consumers because they will generally receive more offers of products and services in which they are likely to have interest. This saves the brands advertising money and decreases the user's aggravation of getting unwanted messages. Everyone wins.

It is very important to know that the brands do not send the perks to users. That could be a violation of privacy. Klout is the necessary connecting point in the middle between vendors connecting with Klout users. Brands do not know who the recipients of specific Klout perks are. Klout does not make e-mail addresses or any other identifying information available to the brands out of their respect for the privacy of Klout users.

A critical part of the perk program that Klout offers is that no one is obligated to only make complimentary comments about the brand from which they receive the perk. In fact, they don't even have to write anything about it. Jon Dick said it very well when he told us, "If you are not in the pocket of someone, you have more credibility."[12] It would only erode the credibility that Klout has if it required users to say something nice about a product or even forced them to reply in order to earn the perk. Klout stands in the middle between the brand offering the perk and the user receiving it. By setting up guidelines that honor and respect each party in the transaction, Klout brings together two parties who can benefit each other.

This is a trend we see developing as more brands choose to target heavy social media users hoping for positive mentions among these key influencers.

Natt Garun wrote in Digital Trends about a nightclub in Los Angeles that gives special treatment to members active in Klout. Members with scores of 50 and higher can gain entrance to the Playhouse Nightclub in Hollywood and receive VIP treatment on the house.[13]

Klout mentioned this subject on its blog:

> *What's also interesting for us at Klout is the entertainment industry's quick adoption of Crimson Hexagon's technology to help place a value on the social presence of celebrities and would-be celebrities. The entertainment industry is increasingly looking at Klout as a social resume for their clientele, using it as a factor in making casting and hiring decisions. The industry will now have that critical influence data baked into one of their favorite monitoring tools.[14]*

Once a key influencer receives a perk, he or she has the option (but not the obligation) of discussing it on a public forum like Facebook, Twitter, or another platform. At that point, the brand could reach out to the influencer if it recognizes signals in social media. The transaction would then shift to the choice of the influencer and the brand for making connection and sharing contact information.

Jon Dick mentioned that the concept of brands working with key influencers is not new. He talked about the practice that Procter & Gamble has used in its marketing through the years to connect with baseball coaches, who are influential at a very local level, to become advocates and influencers.

Today, Procter & Gamble is involved with TREMOR. According to TREMOR's web page:

> TREMOR™ *is the word-of-mouth marketing organization developed by Procter & Gamble that combines P&G's wide-ranging marketing expertise with key learnings from cognitive science. TREMOR is a leader in applying these learnings to the idea of consumer advocacy as the driving force behind effective, measurable word-of-mouth marketing campaigns.*
>
> *A TREMOR campaign creates consumer-to-consumer conversations on a national scale that deliver measurable results using quantitative and qualitative measures of effectiveness. TREMOR is a complete end-to-end marketing solution that includes intensive consumer research, message development and campaign execution. The disruptive message serves as a discussion trigger to launch consumer advocacy through a network of more than 500,000 highly connected moms. With TREMOR, an effective, targeted message about your brand can be amplified through waves of consumer advocacy.*[15]

What Procter & Gamble is doing is indicative of where social media is today. Klout is leveraging this desire to further connect with people. That is why we believe that Klout is more than just a score. It is a new way of using social media and today's technology in order to connect with people in an authentic way.

Brands that choose to remain in the "spray and pray" mode of marketing will not be as effective. The marketplace today is changing. Consumers are looking for real people at companies with whom they can identify. It is much like the frustration that people have expressed when they are in "voice mail hell." Sometimes we want to talk with a real live human, and social media allows us to have that human connection.

This doesn't mean that broadcasting is dead. There still is a place for television, radio, newspaper, magazines, and other forms of mass communication advertising. However, brands must recognize that the world has changed. People want to connect with brands at a human level. Those brands that recognize this and implement appropriate policies will succeed. Just like it has been throughout history, those who remain locked into what worked in the past, and what doesn't work today, will fail.

In a recent discussion on our Facebook page about *Klout Matters*, Michelle Colon-Johnson agreed when we said that the Internet is shifting to more and more emphasis on people with genuine, authentic connections: "I agree one hundred percent; it is for sure The Go-Giver mentality! Building authentic relationships that turn into not only relationships, but quality ones that are in the end very profitable for everyone in the relationship. Because we do business with those whom we know, like, and trust, we are influenced by the same."[16]

Carly Alyssa Thorne, a speaker and consultant who is passionate about social media, gave this advice about the importance of being authentic: "Be authentic across all platforms. Show the different aspects of your personal life, home life, and business life. Show your passions, hobbies, work, values, and be the same as you are on stage, if you are speaking, as when you get off stage. Engage with fans on your [Facebook] pages."[17]

Klout's practice of working with key influencers is at the core of its strategy. Yes, this practice has been used for centuries to create goodwill with key influencers. Today, Klout is using this time-honored concept to make better connections between ultimate buyers and vendors. It is that "advocate" that we have mentioned before.

To support this further, Nielson related a survey where it found that 92 percent of consumers trust what they hear from friends and family. According to Nielsen's latest Global Trust in Advertising report, which surveyed more than 28,000 Internet respondents in 56 countries, 92 percent of consumers around the world say they trust earned media, such as recommendations from friends and family, above all other forms of advertising—an increase of 18 percent since 2007. Online consumer reviews are the second most trusted source of brand information and messaging, with 70 percent of global consumers surveyed online indicating they trust messages on this platform, an increase of 15 percent in four years.

The survey also showed that nearly 6 in 10 global online consumers (58 percent) trust messages found on company websites, and half trust e-mail messages that they signed up to receive. On the web, 4 in 10 respondents rely on ads served alongside search engine results, 36 percent trust online video advertisements, and one-third believe the messages in online banner ads—an increase of 27 percent since 2007. Sponsored ads on social networks, a new format included in the 2011 Nielsen survey, are credible among 36 percent of global respondents.[18]

This is not surprising. People trust the words of those they admire much more than a paid advertisement. Klout is focusing on this time-honored relationship. We predict that we'll see more brands developing relationships with those who meet certain criteria, whether that be a Klout Score or some other qualifying test.

CHAPTER 8

What You Can Do When You Don't Have Time for Social Media

The secret to success is good leadership, and good leadership is all about making the lives of your team members or workers better.
—TONY DUNGY

Time is a funny thing. It can fly, run out, and be up. It can be spent, killed, and passed. It will tell and it is money. With all of these amazing things time does, people never seem to actually have any of it!
—BENNY LEWIS

One of the biggest complaints that people have about social media is that they don't have enough time to do it properly. Let's face it— we're all busy today with so much going on in our lives we don't have time for any unproductive activities. We would submit that doing social media, or any other business activity, needs to focus on those activities that result in desired goals and outcomes. Using social media to research new business, stay in touch with important people, and ultimately to increase the bottom line is a great activity to pursue! Social media, when done properly, is very productive and needed for today's business professional.

In this chapter we will share insights as to what successful people are doing to enhance not only their social media activity but more important their business. We will also take a look at specific tools that can help you to do more with your social media work.

Years ago when social media was making its entrance into the world, many people felt that posting on Facebook or sending tweets was a hideous waste of time. But as they saw social media emerge more and more as a prominent way of marketing and exerting influence, they realized they needed to spend some time learning how to use it.

The challenge is real. We do have many activities that consume our time today as thought leaders. We need to educate ourselves on what's happening in the world and in our fields. We need to listen to podcasts that enrich our minds and help us to learn. We need to watch educational videos on YouTube and on other platforms that help us to maintain our degree of influence. After all, if you're going to be a thought leader you need to focus on creating wonderful ideas, and this usually comes from reading what others are doing. None of us lives in a vacuum, and even if we did, we wouldn't be able to come up with very valuable compelling content.

So how do you handle it all? How can you manage tasks that are required to create compelling content and then tell others about it on social media? Unfortunately there is no one right answer. It is an ongoing work in progress to figure out how to manage our time and where to invest our time most wisely.

Alexandra Samuel wrote a post for *Harvard Business Review* where she discussed the importance of making space for social media. Three of the questions she recommended that social media users should embrace include:

1. What am I learning from social media?
2. Who am I meeting through social media?
3. Who am I reaching through social media?[1]

These questions, and others, can help to focus your efforts so that you get the best return from the time and effort spent on online tasks. The Internet is well known as a time waster, if not used properly. Having the right questions for you and your needs will help to focus your efforts into those areas that yield the best results.

There are some specific tasks we can undertake that can help us better manage the timing demands of work, particularly as they relate to social media. To research this we talked with a number of people who are very successful in business and who are successful in social media.

All of this can help you to boost and maintain a higher Klout Score by engaging in the right activities in the right way.

Recently, Terry put together a program called Time Management for Social Media in which he shared many ideas and gems on how to increase your effectiveness using principles of time management as applied to social media. Many of those ideas will be illustrated here along with some additional material. If you are interested in that program and some of the concepts that are unique to it, you can go to http://smtm.TerryBrock.com/llufsmtm.

Business-Building (and Klout Score–Building) Tips and Techniques

Like any other endeavor in life, achieving success with social media and in boosting your Klout Score requires a system. Without a system you are not able to achieve what is necessary to get ahead in life. Developing those systems for achievement are critical in life. In fact, that is why Terry created his corporation in the early 1980s called Achievement Systems Inc.

You have a strong competitive advantage and are more likely to succeed if you have an efficient system that helps you get important tasks done on any endeavor. This chapter in the book can be worth the investment of your time, money, and effort by itself. Here are some specific steps you can take that include tactics and principles that will help you to manage your social media better, get more business, and raise your Klout Score. By following these steps, you'll be able to (1) clarify your thinking about what you want to do in your business and your life, (2) focus your activities in those areas that can generate the best benefits for you, (3) build your business into what you want it to be, (4) boost your Klout Score and influence, and (5) maintain a higher Klout Score.

1. Clearly Define Your Purpose

This is no mystery. It is the first step you have to take on any venture in order to be successful. If you don't clearly know where you are headed and what you are intending to accomplish, you will wander aimlessly from one "exciting new idea" to another. In today's fast-changing world, it is easy to be distracted.

You have to clearly state what it is you want before you can achieve it. Napoleon Hill was the master of this. He helped millions of people find out what they need to do and how to do it. He called this the definiteness of purpose. This was the first important principle in his classic bestselling book, *Think and Grow Rich*. Until you have clarified what you want and put on blinders to block anything else that gets in the way, you will be hopelessly battered back and forth between the new shiny objects of the moment.

If you are a thought leader, think about what you want to be known for. There are lots of thought leaders out there, and our world needs them today. What is your niche? Where do you want to excel? This should be based on a number of factors:

- **Your level of competency in a given field**. You must have an exceptional skill level that provides a lot of value for people in today's marketplace. This usually comes from experience and education. For us, the formal education route worked very well. However, we are increasingly seeing more and more people who did not take a formal education and who have educated themselves by reading voraciously and attending seminars and learning constantly. In today's highly competitive world, you must integrate lifelong learning as a critical component of living. Terry likes to say you not only need lifelong learning, but you need daylong learning—learn something new every day to stay relevant in today's world.
- **The level of demand for that skill**. You might be the world's leading expert on fifteenth-century tsetse flies in Ethiopia. (Okay, just go with it for a moment!) Yet, you have to step back and think about how much the market needs that information, how much people value it, and how much the world is willing to pay for it. Some will say, "Do what your heart tells you, and the money will follow." We don't necessarily agree with

that philosophy. You have to find out what people in the market are looking for because, after all, they are the ones who will be paying for your knowledge. Many people have done what they love and the money did not follow. This is cold, hard reality. Find an area where people want and are ready, willing, and able to pay you for your expertise. Often this will require adding additional skill sets. Be willing to pay the price in terms of reading extra books, listening to extra podcasts, attending college courses, or whatever it takes to become the person you want to be.

- **How easily you can be replaced.** This is an area that people don't like to address. We all have skill levels in life, and the market values those to a certain extent. No one is saying that one person is inherently worth more than another person. However, certain skill sets are worth a lot more than others. For instance, a janitor is just as valuable as a human being as a brain surgeon. Both people are cherished as human beings. Yet few would disagree that the brain surgeon should be paid more in money than the person who has only the competency to do janitorial work. Also, we can replace the janitor much faster and easier than we can replace the brain surgeon. To become a brain surgeon requires many years of arduous training and skill development. You can't replace a brain surgeon overnight, but a janitor can literally be replaced overnight for the skill of being a janitor.

Always consider these three areas before you embark on a new venture and when defining your purpose in business. Some people might have other ideas and believe that they should simply follow what they love and not worry about the ramifications of business. The real world can be cruel and hard. The reality is that life consists of certain principles that work and certain principles that don't work. Your job to be successful is to determine what principles work and apply those in the activities that you perform.

Life is not fair. This is something that a successful person realizes after a while. You can achieve what you want in life if you apply the success principles to your life and abstain from those principles that inevitably lead to failure. This should be the goal of every thought leader. Find the key principles of success in whatever endeavor you engage in. Relentlessly force yourself to do the right things that can contribute to and bring you the results you want. At the same time, discipline yourself to refrain from those activities that detract from getting the results you want.

This principle works in social media just like it does in the rest of life. Make it your goal to be a scientist of sorts. Scientifically find out what works and what does not work. Step back from the emotion of the moment and focus on what you can do to achieve the goals that you want. This discipline will pay with rewards for you, not only in your work with social media, but also in life.

All of this relates to your Klout Score, but more important, to how you are going to succeed in business. By applying principles that work consistently in business you will inevitably be able to raise your Klout Score.

2. Find Those Platforms Where Your Needs Are Met

An old saying is if you want to catch bass, you've got to go where the bass are. Where do your buyers hang out? What communities or tribes should you be most involved in on a regular basis? Often we find that in today's professional world you need to be in a few carefully selected tribes for maximum success.

Many thought leaders find that they need to be in two key tribes. One of those is their professional organization where they gain new knowledge and interface with colleagues who can help them to learn new ideas. For us we have found that the National Speakers Association, along with its accompanying chapters around the United States and affiliate organizations in other countries, has helped us to gain an enormous amount of knowledge and information. Not only are we able to acquire the technical and professional expertise we need, but we have also found that we have been able to establish some of the best long-term relationships with other people anywhere. Find the community or tribe that works best for you in your particular thought leader area.

A second type of community or tribe you want to be around will be those who are buyers. If you can establish a very good relationship and be part of the community, then those in that community will see you as someone who is contributing, not just trying to sell your services. Find those areas where you can make a contribution in a significant way.

You gain influence—hence enhance your Klout Score—when people respect you and view you as someone who is highly influential. You want to carefully select those few tribes or communities where you can be actively involved.

You can't be involved in every organization. This is where you'll use judgment and experimentation. You want to try various tribes or communities to see which work best for you. Determine which have more value and professional expertise with the membership. We have found it best to avoid very small groups where there are not many people associated and you don't gain very much professionally. Focus your efforts into groups where you can reap the maximum value for your input of time, money, and effort.

Become known as a person who is contributing regularly and giving back to a larger community. In doing this you increase your influence and you increase the number of people who look to you for advice and want to do business with you.

Social media writer Miriam Solzberg offered these ideas on how to build community on an individual basis:

> *Whenever you connect with someone new in your networks, especially Facebook, make it a habit to welcome that person just by saying something as simple as "so glad to connect with you and looking forward to learning more about you." It means a lot to the individual that you just connected with because it shows that he or she is not just another number in your network. It shows you care, and that alone will encourage later on more engagement with that individual which will go a long way in the end.[2]*

One of the best ways to contribute to any community is to enable others in that community. This is a time-honored principle of being with people. You get ahead when you help others get ahead. Constantly be on the lookout for ways that you can enhance someone else's business and help people to achieve the goals they want. As you do this you will become the person who people want to be around. You will become the person whose content people will want to consume. If people find value from reading your blog posts, watching your videos, and listening to your podcasts, they will want to be around you. All of this will help to enhance your credibility and increase your engagement with your community.

In a video interview, Terry spoke with J. B. Glossinger, the host of the podcast *Morning Coach*. This is the number one–rated podcast in the world for self-help and personal development. J.B. said that he has over 60,000 people who regularly are in a Facebook group. This community is a great way to stay in touch and let members get to know each other.[3]

Glossinger said that he uses social media as a tool and doesn't aim for a given number (such as a Klout Score) or even for a specific number of followers or friends. Instead he is interested in building a community which he does on Facebook in a private group. As he put it, using these tools "takes the relationship to an extremely high level." This is what community and social media are all about. Klout provides that direction to know what to do to interact in a socially responsible and beneficial way in the world of social media. You can catch the full video with J. B. Glossinger at http://KloutMatters.com/videos-and-more. You can also reach this site by scanning the following QR code with your smartphone.

It really goes back to what our mothers told us long ago. It is important to be kind to others and to find ways that you can help them. Our mothers might not have worked much with Klout Scores—or any social media for that matter! However, the principles that they taught us about helping others and being there to genuinely care for others still apply in our hectic-paced world of social media today.

Experimentation is an important part of this process. You will find you need to test several groups to make sure you're in the right one. As associations are comprised of human beings who come and go, you will find they are constantly morphing and changing throughout time.

Terry has been in the National Speakers Association since 1988, and he has seen many changes over the decades in that organization. It is good for professionals and thought leaders to continually reevaluate where it is best to expend our time, money, and effort.

View yourself as a scientist who is constantly searching to find out what works best for this vital area of your life. To be successful today it is essential that you have strong, ongoing education along with a supportive community.

Our friend Harvey Mackay has written several *New York Times* bestseller books, including *Swim with the Sharks Without Being Eaten Alive, Beware the Naked Man Who Offers You His Shirt,* and others. Mackay says that you need more than one tribe. For instance, you might have one community or tribe where you learn skills in swimming, if that is something that's important to you. Then you might have another tribe that helps with your spiritual needs at your church, synagogue, mosque, or other place of spiritual pursuit. In addition to that you might have another tribe that is in your local community. There is no set number that fits for every person. You have to find out what works best for you. We have found that having between three and five tribes works best. Focus more of your activity into two or three of those tribes and visit other tribes only on an occasional basis.

3. Know That You Have to Spend Time on Social Media

This is something that you need to continually tell yourself. As a busy thought leader you don't have time to waste. You have to invest your time, money, and effort where it is going to pay off with the best results for you. Social media is critical today. Some think it is still very frivolous. We just hope that those people are our competitors!

You have to continually remind yourself of the importance of putting quality time into social media. That means you contribute value by creating content and by helping others.

Firmly know that you need to spend time on social media on a regular basis. Successful millionaires whom we have spoken with, who created millions from their work in social media, have said that they devote a specific time each day to be there and to respond to people. This is not a matter of sending out broadcasts and hoping that you'll turn Twitter into the twenty-first-century version of the 1960s television commercial campaign. If all you're doing is broadcasting and you're not engaging with customers, you're in trouble. A keyword for social media involvement today is engagement.

Building success in social media, and building your Klout Score, is a matter of responding to others. Lisa Jimenez, a success coach, puts it well: "Respond to posts and comments. Social media can do a lot for us, but it still cannot build the relationship!"[4] Her point is that social media must be viewed as a part of a successful relationship-building set of tools. Social media is strong and necessary in today's world; however, don't rely only on it to build the solid, meaningful relationships you need. You can see the video with Lisa Jimenez at http://KloutMatters.com/videos-and-more. You can also reach this site by scanning the following QR code with your smartphone.

We are continually impressed with the benefits that come from physically being at a meeting or convention. Yes, we both use social media extensively, almost every day. Yet, we find that a relationship takes a jump in benefits for both parties when you have a meal together, attend a conference together, or even have that chance meeting in the hall. Let social media be a part of all you do, and remember to physically "be there" at critical meetings.

Always remind yourself of the importance of spending time with social media and engaging with others in a valuable way for them. We've seen clients of ours in the past who thought that all they needed to do was to send out X number of tweets per day and they were involved with social media. Inevitably these people either had to change and engage with their customers or they became frustrated with social media and walked away saying something like "this stuff doesn't work."

Gina Rau discussed this on Quora:

The best advice is to grow a loyal fanship of customers or fans of your brand that truly want to engage with your brand—not fans that just want the one time deal. Continue to share good content that is a mix of yours and curated content that educates, entertains or informs. Ask questions of your fanship to better understand them, and get them to engage. Encourage participation always![5]

Social media, and raising your Klout Score, really involves engagement. This is not something you can hire out. It is something that you personally must do. Yes, you can and should hire out certain elements of it. For instance, sending out regular messages with your legacy content is something that can be hired out to an outside service. However, you have to be involved in answering and engaging with people who respond to you. It could be a good idea to work with services like Elance, oDesk, and others where you can hire a subcontractor to help with some specific tasks.

We have found a lot of success and regularly work with people we have hired through oDesk (oDesk.com). This has freed our time to pursue those other tasks that only we can do. Think about how you can outsource a lot of tasks that would be better done by someone else. This is smart business. This is smart time management.

Focus on doing those important tasks that only you can do. We wish we would have said this first, but Peter Drucker is the thought leader here. That great management guru told us that we should always focus on doing those tasks that only we can do.

For many thought leaders today, that means focusing on learning. Reading and studying become an integral part of what you do each day. Creating content that is compelling is also widely important. This is something that every front leader should do on a regular basis. It's all right to work with others to help create that content. In fact, it is a wise idea to work in collaboration with others as you create material. Your content can become too insular if you only rely on what you know. Just be sure to do those things that only you can do.

In addition to learning, a big part of your job is your direct contact with key buyers. As a thought leader you need to continually market your skills and services. Marketing is something that you cannot neglect. You will also need to take an active role in it even if you bring in others to assist. Sometimes the most effective way to connect is with personal contact.

This personal contact can take the form of a quick phone call, a hello at a regular connection meeting, or some other physical meeting like a lunch or dinner. We've never ceased to be amazed that even with all the great technology, a face-to-face, live, in-person meeting is sometimes the most powerful. In fact, very wise thought leaders strategically use physical meetings to gain a competitive advantage. When you can look at people across the lunch table and talk to them about matters that are going to help them, you gain a tremendous advantage over a competitor who might merely be sending an e-mail.

Another area that is becoming increasingly important in our technology age is making your own video. Video is a powerful tool for creating a connection with important people. A tool like Eyejot, which is mentioned in Chapter 9, is a powerful way for you to connect with people one-on-one. This is something that you need to do yourself.

A lot is being done today through video with tools like Skype and Google+ Hangouts, Eyejot, and many other tools for communicating. If you find it very difficult to communicate via video, this is an area where you would be well advised to consider a coach to help you with some basics on how to communicate. Be sure to check the appendixes of this book for a treasure trove of information on tools that can help you.

These are some of the examples where you need to be involved, and doing this will help to increase your marketing effectiveness and thereby increase your Klout Score.

Trying to farm out all your social media activity to another would be like hiring someone to pass out your cards at a Chamber of Commerce networking event. Anyone who tried that would be looked upon in an extremely unfavorable way—and rightly so.

Remind yourself continually that you need to spend time with social media in the right way to build your business—and this will build your Klout Score.

4. Be a Great Resource for Others

In today's hyper-competitive world, we do not lack for information. What we really need is trusted advisors who can help us to decipher the clutter of information and know what is best. If you can position yourself as a trusted advisor in a given field, you will have a loyal following.

Do an experiment on this yourself. Think of five top influential people in a given field. Go over to Klout.com and track what their Klout Scores are today. Then track that over a period of a week to two weeks.

Write and blog about important events in your industry. Write material that is evergreen that helps people in a particular field. This is all about building your street credibility (street cred).

One of our favorite bloggers is Srinivas Rao, who runs the podcast Blogcast.fm. When we asked him about a strategy for networking in social media, he responded with some keen insights for a person just getting started: "Create an inner circle of people who mention you on Twitter. Focus on interacting with them for several weeks. That's more useful than inflating your follower numbers."[6]

Lisa Jimenez is a success coach who helps people overcome limiting beliefs. She started using social media about two years ago and has already earned a healthy Klout Score—and bottom-line revenue as a result. She has used Facebook pictures a lot and regularly encourages others to become better. She describes how she did this in more detail in the video that accompanies this book, which you can view at http://KloutMatters.com/videos-and-more.

Writing is a great way to do this. People love to read about important information that will affect their lives. If you can write about what is happening and let people in a given niche know that you are discussing this, you can achieve a following. Then, why not give yourself an advantage? Today you can use tools like audio and video to further amplify a written message. When you use audio and video, it moves the communication to a whole new level. If you are known as someone who leverages video, for instance, then you will be able to build a loyal following in a given area. If you're going to use video, make sure that you use it for something that is added value that your audience can't get from text alone.

For instance, if you're going to show how to use a new widget, then use a video so that you can bring in motion and show a much richer and full-dimensional illustration of what can be done with the new widget. In Terry's work in the past with people in the plumbing, heating, and air-conditioning business, he found some who use video to gain a competitive edge. When a new faucet is released, sometimes a video describes much better what it can do than simple words on the screen. Even still pictures don't do justice to motion and movement like a video can.

Using the right media in the right way can give you a significant advantage positioning yourself as a thought leader in a given industry. Make it your goal to be the trusted resource in your community where people eagerly await your new blog posts, videos, audios, and messages that can help them to resolve their problems. Doing this on a regular, weekly basis is a very good idea. Consider doing it more than once a week if that works in your industry.

You want to be a source of valuable information to others. As a thought leader, people will turn to you for ideas, inspiration, and motivation. This means you need to continually feed your own well with good quality information to learn how you can be a better resource for others.

Another way you can do this is to curate certain information. You don't want to only send your own content. Find other articles, videos, and audios that are particularly helpful to your target market. Share these with your community. Be the one who introduces the community to this new content. You want to be seen as the resource people turn to for information.

When Terry was in his MBA program, he was able to take a marketing course with Tom Stanley. At the time, Tom Stanley was a marketing professor at Georgia State University in Atlanta, Georgia. He later went on to write several books about millionaires and how to become a millionaire. One of the books he coauthored with William D. Danko was entitled *The Millionaire Next Door*. Tom Stanley, or as Terry always refers to him, "Dr. Stanley," is a genius on what it takes to become influential and successful.

One of the things that Dr. Stanley reminded us was to be the hub of information or the resource people want to turn to for ideas and references. For instance, you might not be a Realtor, but if someone asks for a good Realtor on the north side of town and you know three good professional Realtors on the north side of town, you will be viewed very favorably. You don't have to be the best dentist in town to know who good dentists are so that you can make those recommendations as well. You get the idea. It is important for you to have a network where you are in the middle of a lot of information and people turn to you for help.

Without even knowing it, and definitely without stating it, Dr. Stanley knew the key to increasing your Klout Score: be the influencer who others turn to. Clients like to be around those who initiate action on the part of others. This is what the influencer does. You want to be the person whom people look to and value enormously. This means you need to know specific knowledge about topics that are important to people in your community.

This goes way beyond gaming some system. It means that you're contributing serious value to other people's lives by helping them in ways that are needed by them in a given moment. Doing this over a sustainable period of time is the best way to ensure not only your higher Klout Score but your ultimate business success.

This relates to the quote from Tony Dungy at the beginning of this chapter. What Tony said about leadership is true of social media success. Make it your goal to see others be successful. Tony has done this all his life.

Terry grew up near Jackson, a small town in lower mid-Michigan. At the time, there was a high school in Jackson named Parkside High School. Terry read about a star football player at Parkside High who was known as not only an outstanding football player, but a model student in academics. This person was Tony Dungy. Through his career and his life, Tony Dungy has been known as a person who helps others achieve their goals. His success with Super Bowl champions the Indianapolis Colts in Super Bowl XLI showed his ability to bring out the best in his players and others.

Think of yourself as a leader who can help others grow and become what they want to be. Think of how you can help them in social media. This will help you and, yes, your own Klout Score. But don't do good for others solely because you're expecting that you'll somehow get that positive kickback. We don't know how, but somehow the world works in a way that if you give and genuinely help others, good comes to you. Tony Dungy was, and is an example of how to "do life right." Thank you, Tony Dungy, for providing an example for us.

5. Provide a Unique Point of View

We, as human beings, value different subjects in different ways. We want to be unique. If you have a blog, for instance, that is a great way to disseminate your information and content. In fact, we feel that a blog should be the center of the thought leader's marketing and social media outreach.

In your blog, you want to give information that is unique, fresh, and from a different perspective than people can hear otherwise. This builds influence and subsequently can build your business and your Klout Score.

Provide a unique point of view on hot issues in your community. Read the other blogs and trade journals that are in your niche, but don't necessarily embrace everything that is being said. Find unique ways in which you can express a different point of view or something that is not seen where everyone else is speaking.

This is basic marketing.

You don't want to be the four thousandth person to say the same thing that they've heard before. Why would they need to hire you if you don't have any extra value to add than the other 3,999 people applying for that job? Be creative and add massive amounts of value to what you offer your target market. This is true for thought leaders as well as anyone who is looking to be hired in a job.

6. Continue to Learn and Grow

One of the most important skills that any thought leader can develop today is how to learn. You are a person who sends information to others. This helps to build your Klout Score as more people are attracted to your message. You have to continue to feed your mind and learn new material.

One of the best ways to learn to continue and grow is by physically attending conferences. Something magical happens when you get around a group of people who think similarly to you or think differently from you. Today's conferences, seminars, workshops, and other gatherings are very good for this. You want to be continually feeding your mind with good, upbeat information and tools that help you to solve problems in your target market.

Of course online learning also is critical. There are wonderful sources of learning available today through webinars, teleseminars, and more online learning. Make it a regular part of your intellectual diet to acquire new information on a daily basis. You cannot afford to fall behind. As you continue to keep your mind alert and abreast of new ideas, you'll be able to add more value to the content that you create. As you create compelling content you will attract more people, which will drive your Klout Score higher.

Be controversial. Be unique. Come up with your own point of view. This is what helps to create a loyal following. As a thought leader, you have an opportunity to understand what's going on in the marketplace, synthesize that in your brain based on your experience, and deliver a point of view that is unique and refreshing to your marketplace. Make sure that what you say solves problems that your community cannot get solved any other place.

As you do this and build a reputation for being a person with your own unique point of view, people will not only come to your site to read what you say but they will also tell others. A critical part of building your influence—and hence your Klout Score—is to have others talk about what you're doing so that the viral effect will take place.

Jeffrey Hayzlett, a marketing speaker, author, and past chief marketing officer for Kodak, told us that he uses viral marketing and shared some insights into what works:

> *Viral content is a great example of friendsourcing, a personal and more trusted version of crowdsourcing. People will watch videos, view photos and read blogs that their friends recommend, so it's very important to have and appeal to growing communities on social channels.*
>
> *You also need to understand who your targeted audience is and what they're watching/viewing/reading. I launch a very specific call to action in most posts as a means to leverage the engagement with my communities.[7]*

You want your messages to go viral. You want your messages to be so good that people want to share them with others, and then their friends want to share them with their old friends, and so on and so on. This word-of-mouth advertising has been and always will be the best form of advertising.

7. Forget the Old "Spray and Pray"

This is a phrase from long ago in marketing, advertising, and public relations. The concept was that if you did enough broadcasting of your message to enough people (we never found out an exact number of what "enough" really was!) you would eventually find success.

The most successful marketers and thought leaders today engage with their communities through relevant, compelling conversations. They talk with, not at, them to get ideas. In fact, the best thought leaders are those who ask more questions and solicit more from their community than they tell. They listen. They acknowledge their community. They involve their community in discussions.

Andrea Vahl is a social media consultant, speaker, and coauthor of *Facebook Marketing All-in-One for Dummies*. We asked her about how today's social media world is different from the "spray and pray" that was used in the past. She responded: "To be effective on social media, you have to talk with people. You can't just broadcast your links or news. It's just like any in-person networking you do—ask about them, be interested in people, and if you can help them in some way, your business will benefit."[8]

This is what the best thought leadership is about today, and it is what leads to higher influence and ultimately higher Klout Scores.

Since social media is about engaging with people in meaningful conversations much more than broadcasting a staid, boring message, it is time for a mind change. We have to embrace community and engagement more than spewing out a bunch of propaganda.

Challenge yourself to embrace this new way of connecting with people and you'll find a lot more success—and a higher Klout Score!

8. Build a Team

Let's face it, in today's world there is so much to do with social media that one person cannot keep up with it all. If you try to manage all of your accounts in Twitter, Facebook, LinkedIn, YouTube, StumbleUpon, Reddit, Digg, or whatever the other tools are, you are going to be overwhelmed! A thought leader trying to operate alone quickly discovers that it is impossible to get everything done that "should" be done.

However, the real good news is that you don't have to operate alone. Because of the improvements in technology—specifically with bandwidth—you can tap into the services of brilliant people around the world. These brilliant people are virtual assistants, subcontractors, and other people who can work for you and get specific tasks done a lot cheaper than you can do them yourself. You can tap into these people who are experts at writing, at assembling video, creating graphics, and doing websites much easier than you can do it yourself.

The marketplace and social media have changed significantly in just the past couple of years. Long ago (that's two years ago in social media!) you used to be able to do it on your own. Today the marketplace is changed. You need to build a team around you that can help you to organize all the various components of social media.

Some of these components include (1) creation of content, (2) promotion of your content, and (3) ongoing marketing of your presence on social media. To do all of this properly requires a coordinated, organized system that operates whether you feel like doing it or not. Yes, this is a business and you need to treat it that way. For a solo practitioner or thought leader operating alone, this is a major step forward.

Some of the elements that you want to consider would be in your content creation, making sure that you have ideas sent to you that can serve as springboards for you to create your content. Content creation is something that you cannot outsource. Oh yes, you can try to use a ghostwriter for much of the work, but that's not really you saying it. A ghostwriter can be very helpful to give you initial ideas and a framework for your content, but ultimately *you* need to write your own content.

Once you have your content created in the form of text, audio, and/or video, then you can leverage a team of virtual assistants and subcontractors to help you disseminate the information. This is where you can get a lot more done than you would be able to do on your own. We like to go back to the words of Peter Drucker in the brilliant management and personal development information that he gave us.

In a blog post for The Build Network, the post's author quoted Peter Drucker saying that executives should do what only they can do—create jobs.[9] Throughout his distinguished career, Drucker often spoke of the importance of doing what only you can do and outsourcing the rest.

The content you create should be based on the information that you have from your formal education as well as your ongoing education as we've discussed here. You need to spend personal time learning every day by reading the right blogs, listening to the right podcasts, and watching the right videos. You also need to create your content by attending the right seminars and lectures and conferences in your field. You need to be an authority who has credibility, not just someone who can repurpose the content of others.

Once you've created this content, you get the team to help you send it out to others. This means that you have a team of people who are helping you to format according to your predesign ideas and have that team implement the instructions to send out your content.

For instance, if you do a lot of blogging, you should be the one who initially writes the content. Once it is written, send it to someone who is competent in spellchecking, grammar checking, proofreading, and examining the essence of what you've written. A good source for this would be recent college graduates who majored in English or journalism. Many of these people are brilliant and know their skill and their craft very well. Another great source would be those who are being laid off in the field of journalism now. They are looking for work, even temporary work. If you can find someone who is particularly good at writing and can help you to punch up your writing to make it better, that could be a real asset to you in today's social media world.

Of course, if you can punch out more compelling content, that is going to increase the number of followers you have, and it will enhance your influential impressions on others. If you do that on a consistent basis, then your Klout Score will go up naturally.

If you're using audio or video, make sure that you have a good editor that can edit out the fillers (such as "er" and "um") to help you sound more professional. This is actually very easy to do if you have even a limited knowledge of audio editing tools. One that we often use is called Audacity. It is a free, open-source software that is excellent for editing audio for your podcasts. You can find out more about this at the Audacity website, http://audacity.sourceforge.net. Audacity is available for both Windows and Mac. If you need to learn some special techniques on how to use it, you can find these readily available in YouTube videos and other sources throughout the net.

If you don't want to take the time and make the effort to learn Audacity or another audio editing tool, then it is very easy to find some wonderful high school or college students who use the program and are delighted to help you do editing for a nominal charge. For many executives and thought leaders, it is much better to develop a style or system that they want to use. They concentrate only on recording the raw audio, then send it to an editor who can do the edits based on their predesigned ideas.

This principle particularly applies to video production and editing. For many executives who we coach, we recommend that they focus on how to look good in front of the camera. We also recommend they do not focus on video editing as their time is much too valuable. Yes, a reasonably intelligent thought leader can probably learn how to edit video. However, rather than spending all the time, money, and effort learning how to use video editing, a strong case could be made that your time, money, and effort are much better spent connecting with customers. If you hire someone who can work for a much lower hourly rate while you focus on the higher income-generating activity, we think you would get a thumbs-up from Peter Drucker!

For much of his coaching and communication work, Terry records the raw video and then uploads it to a site where a video editor can download and do the editing per his instructions. Terry took time to develop a system and trained the people who do the video editing for him.

Now that the system is working, Terry is able to generate content and focus on developing compelling content through video interviews that he puts on his website. Yes, he still needs to oversee and make adjustments to various videos from time to time. However, this is a much better use of his resources and time then doing all the video editing himself.

Much more can be said about building your virtual team through virtual assistance and other services. Services like oDesk.com, Elance.com, and Freelancer.com, among others, are very helpful. We encourage you to explore these various services and find those that are best for you in your particular area.

Serious social media work requires a discipline to treat it like a business. This is the nature of where social media is today versus even a couple of years ago. You will gain a decisive, competitive advantage by developing a finely tuned, well-functioning machine that serves you in the world of social media. Keep making modifications and changes as nothing stays the same in this fast-moving world.

You will be well served if you have a mindset that allows for continual adaptation and modification as you see the world and your marketplace changing. Hold on to principles that work throughout time. Embrace the tools and technologies that come and go as they serve you and fit into your overall strategy.

9. Seek Exposure to New People Who Are Relevant

This is the advice of Paul Kim, VP of marketing with Klout. He told us in an interview that it is important to continually expand your network and get to know people who have a high degree of influence in your community.[10]

People come and go on social media. You see an ebb and flow. That is the way human nature works. You can think of social media much like farming. A farmer has to continually tend to the crops, and it is an ongoing process. When harvest comes, you have to store your best "seed corn" for next year's crop. Social media requires diligence and nurturing to keep it fresh and alive. As you get to know new people who are relevant in your area of choice, your niche, you will remain fresh and alive. You'll be able to experience new thoughts and ideas. This is truer in the area of social media than any other area. We are continually amazed at new developments that come out almost every day. Yes, sometimes it is a challenge to keep up with them all! By constantly bringing new people with fresh ideas into your life, you remain alive and vibrant in a continually changing world. This helps you to create better content and ultimately helps to enhance your own digital influence.

10. Focus on a Specific Niche

This has to be one of the most important activities you can do as a thought leader. You need to find a niche where you have passion and competency. If you only have passion, you won't be able to attract as much of a following because there won't be the depth of expertise. If you only have competency and no passion, then after a while, it gets boring and others will detect that you are bored and leave.

Make sure that the niche you select is large enough to be profitable for business purposes. If you have passion about an area, it does not necessarily mean that the money will flow to you.

The specific niche you want should be one where there are enough people to provide an income for you where you have passion and competency. This combination will help you to be successful.

You can start to find that niche by looking at Facebook pages and studying tweets that are along topics with which you resonate. Find others who are out there and are influential in those areas. Make sure that you focus on areas where you have the passion and the competency and there is a big demand for your skills.

CHAPTER 9

Tools That Can Help You Manage Social Media

Technology is nothing. What's important is that you have a faith in people, that they're basically good and smart, and if you give them tools, they'll do wonderful things with them.
—STEVE JOBS

By now you realize that social media use and participation is vital for your Klout Score to rise. If, at the same time, you're also feeling swamped and having that "How am I ever going to get all this stuff done?" question coming to your mind—then welcome to the party, pal! You need about 72 hours each day to accomplish all that needs to be done with social media!

Well, we can't give you 72 hours each day. If we could do that, we would have a whole lot more opportunities of helping others! However, we can share some tools that can help you get a lot more done in a lot less time. As we talk to many successful social media practitioners, we find that everyone who is doing exceptionally well is using some other tool to leverage his or her ability.

In this chapter, we will share some of those tools that can help you to get more done with social media and hence build more business and help to build your Klout Score.

Keep in mind that in an ever-changing marketplace, there will be new tools that come and go on a regular basis. Also the tools that we use today can be radically changed as the owners of those tools and new features subtract certain features, are bought out by other companies, or simply go out of business. This is the reality of writing a book in today's fast-changing social media world.

Be sure to regularly check our website, http://KloutMatters.com, for more updated information.

Here are some tools that can boost your productivity so that you will be able to accomplish a lot more in a lot less time.

HootSuite

When we asked our contributing experts about their favorite tools for managing social media, HootSuite was the favorite, by far. Like many social media products, HootSuite has a free version and a professional version. Terry uses the free version and has for a long time. Gina has been using the professional version for two years now and is very pleased with it as well.

HootSuite gives you the ability to look at specific streams in social media without the clutter. You might say it is a tool that makes sense of the mess of too much information overload and social media. We use it to keep track of what's going on with various Twitter streams as well as LinkedIn and Facebook information. You can set up a specific command set within HootSuite so that it follows and monitors what select people are doing. This is an excellent way to track what really is going on in your field and to monitor key players who you want to track.

As you're using HootSuite, don't forget about its little brother, Hootlet. Hootlet is a tool that gives you the ability to compress or condense a given URL (web address) so that you're able to send out information without gobbling up your precious 40-character limit in Twitter. Commonly known as a "URL shortener," this is a great tool to have available when you're referencing a number of different websites. Terry used this extensively when he was editor-in-chief for AT&T's Networking Exchange blog. Often he had to refer to many different websites, and using Hootlet gave him the ability to compress those websites so that many more could be shared.

As you progress with HootSuite, be sure to look at some of the professional applications that work with it. These applications are continually changing, so you want to monitor what is current. Some of these give you the ability to work with YouTube, Blogger, Instagram,

Tumblr, Evernote, and many others. Do a quick Google search on "HootSuite applications" to find out what is available currently. You can use this as a "force multiplier" (to use a military phrase) to get more done in less time for your social media work.

Rapportive

Rapportive is a tool that we regularly use with Gmail. It gives the ability to examine many different references to people who are in your Gmail account. One of the best features is that it allows you to see a picture of people who are in your Gmail list, but you might not know what they look like.

Rapportive also lets you see other social media references for given people. For instance, you can find out what they have done recently on Twitter, Facebook, and LinkedIn.

This might seem a little bit creepy at first for those of us who were interested in privacy. However, given that all of this is done only with the permission of those being viewed, it makes more sense.

BufferApp

BufferApp is a tool that lets you schedule your posts and tweets. This is extraordinarily important when you want to send out information over a regular smooth stream rather than clump several hundred messages within one hour. This is particularly useful with Twitter. In Twitter, you might want to send out several tweets that are particularly well scheduled throughout the day.

We have many contacts from our talks in Europe, North America, Asia, and Australia. The time zone differences are always a factor in our business. When using a tool like Buffer (bufferapp.com), we can make sure that certain tweets go out at relevant and convenient times for people around the world. This means we don't have to wake up at three o'clock in the morning just to send out several tweets!

Be aware of the downside of using Buffer or other scheduling tools, however. Facebook has been known to detract from people's

EdgeRank because they have used an outside tool like Buffer or other scheduling tools. If your EdgeRank is dinged a bit because of your use of an outside tool, one might wonder how that will affect your Klout Score. It can to a small extent, according to Ding Zhou, Klout's chief scientist. However, we have found that it is a trade-off between convenience and a slight difference in ranking. We have used Buffer, and still do, because when people respond to a curated post, our own Klout Scores increase.

Scheduling tools like Buffer or Post Planner give you the ability to schedule and manage your outbound communication much better. We have found that posting directly to Facebook is still a good idea. We use direct posting and scheduled posts through Buffer. The most important element is to select content that will resonant with your audience so they respond.

Recently, Buffer announced an alliance with Feedly, a news-reading app. This combination helps you to check out your favorite blogs, news sources, and other reference points on the net and schedule posts telling others about them. This is a powerful tool for thought leaders and can directly help to build your Klout Score.

By curating great content with others, you enhance your position as a thought leader who is the resource to follow. You can build credibility and help others to solve their problems. This combination of Buffer and Feedly can help to make your curation efforts much easier and give you more recognition in the social media world.

Eyejot

Eyejot is a tool that is not officially known as a social media tool. Yet when used properly it can supplement and energize your posts on Facebook, your tweets on Twitter, and messages on LinkedIn. We use this regularly to send out a "Wow!" message every now and then.

Eyejot gives you the ability to record a video of up to five minutes for free. This video is not stored on your computer, nor is it stored on your recipient's computer. It is stored in the cloud, Amazon's S3 servers to be specific. This means that when you send people a video they are not receiving a physical video file (like MOV, WMV, etc.). Instead, they are receiving a reference to a video, like any other external link.

The video plays on their computer. Think of it like clicking on a link to a YouTube video. You don't store that video on your computer. It is stored on YouTube's servers. Since it is using Flash or HTML5 technology, it is accessible even with some of the most aggressive corporate firewalls. And that is okay because it is not downloading any software onto a person's computer.

A handy little trick is to send out a video to a number of people by recording the video to yourself. Then send the code that you have sent to yourself to others who you wish to receive the video. Terry recommends that you use a URL shortener tool like Hootlet (a subset of HootSuite) to make the message more manageable.

Since we are talking about how you can increase business and how you can raise your Klout Score accordingly, Eyejot is a great way to connect with people. You can create a special video and put the code into a Facebook post. This is a quick way to send a video. If you have the higher level of Eyejot videos, you can be notified whenever someone views that video.

Twubs

Twubs is one of our favorites! It is designed to monitor groups that are tweeting about a particular topic by using a tool called a hashtag. The pound sign, # (often called a hashtag), is a great tool to designate a topic for a series of tweets. Terry often uses this when he's speaking at a conference. For instance, if he is speaking for the widget makers conference he might create the hashtag #WMC. After that is created, simply by inserting those particular characters into a tweet, all people at the conference would be able to refer to that with Twubs to understand what others are saying and tweeting about during the conference. This serves as an ongoing journal of some of the best of that conference as determined by those participating.

It is also a great tool for those who cannot attend a particular conference to find out what is going on and what has been said at that conference. By merely referencing that particular hashtag, you can get some of the best parts of that conference, or what was said from the platform, after the fact.

TweetBinder

This is a new tool which collects tweets based around a common hashtag. This product functions similarly to Twubs but its real added benefit is the ability to analyze what was said in the discussion. You can quickly draw graphs with it. How can this help with your Klout Score? As a thought leader, you'll be able to draw more from the data from what people expressed at, for instance, a given event where a hashtag was used. You can find the number of tweets from given people to see who was more vocal. You can track the number of retweets to determine popularity. A tool like this can give a thought leader better analysis of what is going on around a given topic. You can get very specific in your study of a topic. This is one worth investigating!

These and other tools can be very helpful for today's social media–savvy marketer. Whenever you can find a tool that will leverage your ability to do more in less time, it's worth considering. We look forward to hearing from you as you discover new tools when they are released on the market. Please be sure to visit our website for more updated information as new tools are released.

CHAPTER 10

Enhance Your Social Media Presence—and Boost Your Klout Score!

Engage with people on your social channels. Comment.
Ask and answer questions. Like stuff you like.
—MICHAEL BRENNER, VICE PRESIDENT OF
GLOBAL MARKETING, SAP

By now, you've seen that there are no shortcuts to boosting your image in social media. In order to be sustainable, you have to consistently engage with your community. This is much like the real world, where you cannot go to a country club or a Chamber of Commerce, pass out a whole bunch of business cards, and expect to be the hit of the day with one visit. It takes consistent, regular exposure and contribution to the community to make a difference.

The same is true with social media and with building your Klout Score. You have to be there consistently to help people. This means providing value for your readers, listeners, and viewers in social media. You need to consistently provide value. Doing good activities just once in a while will not help. Successful social media users plan their social media content and distribution in a very strategic way.

This does not mean that you should clutter your social media sites with too much information. Some people try to inundate the channel of Twitter, for instance, by posting extraneous information that is not exceptionally valuable. Your goal is to be influential, not noisy.

Here are some specific steps you can take that will help you in the long term to build your social media presence—and thereby increase your Klout Score. We've gathered these from many people who we talked to and interacted with along with our own work online. Use these as starting points to build your own business and become more of the person you want to be online.

Tip 1: Provide Valuable Information

Make it a practice to provide valuable information 90 to 95 percent of the time and sell 5 to 10 percent. Social media has the emphasis on social. It is not "selling media." Of course, businesspeople must, understandably, sell their products and services.

Yet in the world of social media it has been turned upside down. It used to be all selling in business with little information provided. The most successful social media mavens today are those who give a lot of valuable information on a consistent basis. They become a ready resource that many people see as someone whose blog they must read. As you become that resource, you will draw more people to your site like a magnet. If you are only talking about yourself and selling all the time, you are in trouble. Strategically plan to give beneficial ideas to others most of the time, with just enough selling to let them know you are in business.

A much more reliable and attractive way to generate business is to practice giving a lot of value and sell only in a pleasant way. Make offers that people will want in a compelling way, helping them to solve their problems.

Tip 2: Share Stories

Share stories that help people to relate to you. Study your market and your community and find out what challenges they are going through. Then craft stories about how you have been able to help others with similar problems.

Tip 3: Visit Other Sites in Your Community

Make it a point to regularly visit and comment on the sites of other people in your community. They are looking for interaction and participation, so be the first to give it to them. Help them out by being a contributor on their site and bringing value to them. If you do this enough, human nature kicks in and people will want to reciprocate by helping you out. Don't forget you want to encourage people to leave comments on your site and to mention you on major social media platforms. As we are writing this, Klout does not give you any points toward your Klout Score for what you do on your blog. We hope this changes in the future, but you will still help others in a practical way by posting quality content on your blog. As you post quality content on your blog, more people will want to know about it and then will comment on social media platforms like Twitter and Facebook, which are counted toward your Klout Score. These comments in social media platforms like Facebook, Twitter, and LinkedIn, will help to boost your Klout Score.

Tip 4: Talk About Important Events

Talk about important events like the final episode of a TV show or a big sporting event or something else that grabs the attention of a key market. If you talk about this in your online communication, more people will pay attention. Keep it relevant and make sure that you relate directly to the problems and pain that your community is experiencing.

Tip 5: Know Your Visitors

Become genuinely interested in the people who visit your site or your Facebook page, or who send you tweets or partake in other activities on social media. Examine their online presence and find out what areas they are involved in and where they have concerns. Bonus tip: find out areas for which they have a particular passion and find the

areas of commonality you have. It is our belief that we have something in common and something where we disagree with everyone on
the planet. This is human nature. Successful networkers and those
who use the tools of social media properly are those who find areas
of commonality and accentuate them.

We have found that some of the most effective social media mavens
are those who steer clear of controversial topics like politics, religion,
and other "dangerous" areas. Do we have opinions on these topics?
Of course. But a business blog might not be the best place for them.
Be very careful about arguments in social media, which can have
long-term detrimental effects on your business. Any knuckleheads
can argue with people with whom they have disagreements. It takes a
savvy, business-aware marketer and social media guru to know when
to voice personal opinions and when to refrain.

It doesn't mean that you never talk about areas where you would
disagree, but it does mean that you accentuate those areas where you
have agreement, commonality, and mutual benefit.

Tip 6: Get to Know Key Influencers

Embrace the time-honored system of maintaining contact with important people. Harvey Mackay, the author of many *New York Times*
bestseller books, is a master networker. His books, *Swim with the
Sharks without being Eaten Alive* and *Beware the Naked Man Who
Offers You His Shirt*, can help anyone to hone business skills and
networking ability.

Harvey is famous for his Mackay 66 tool. This is a tool that he developed back in the days when pen and paper were common tools for
connecting with people. With the Mackay 66, Harvey would collect
information about people he met over time, learning not only their
name and address but other important information. He developed
a system for collecting and storing vital information on important
contacts. This started with just pen and paper and evolved years ago
into a more sophisticated electronic system.

Information he gathered included where the person went to high
school, where the person went to college, the person's spouse and
children, the interests of the spouse and children, political beliefs, and

many other important details. Harvey encourages people to create their own list of important variables to know about people they meet. Having this information readily available can help build relationships over time.

The Mackay 66 philosophy works better than ever today. In a world where we meet a flurry of people who often have only a superficial knowledge of each other, you can create an advantage for yourself. Visit people's LinkedIn profiles and learn important details about who they are, what they believe, where they went to school, and other vital information.

Add to this other information that you'll collect about people through your study of them. Yes, this will require work. However, it is well worth it when you know specific important features about people to help them solve problems. You will stand out from the crowd and, yes, you will gain more influence this way. And of course, as you build influence you will have the chance to increase and enhance your Klout Score.

The principles that Harvey Mackay has taught for years can help you build your Klout Score. As you get to know key influencers and keep track of their interests, they will notice you. As higher Klout Score holders interact with you, your Klout Score will increase. By combining the tried-and-true principles of connecting with people that Harvey Mackay has been teaching with the power of tools like LinkedIn and other social media platforms, you get the best of both worlds.

Tip 7: Solve Problems

Solving problems requires homework. Find out the key problems that your community is experiencing on a regular basis. Write your blogs, your Facebook posts, your tweets, your LinkedIn posts, and other social media content such that it addresses those problems immediately. For example, if your target market is physicians, you need to be aware that many of them are facing challenges accepting Medicare patients and getting paid much less. You might entitle a blog post, "Should you continue to accept Medicare patients?" That is something that would get the attention of any physician who is wrestling with that dilemma.

Find the key problems in your community and think of ways you can ask a question that will grab attention. Often Terry will speak to many groups around the world on how to better leverage social media and portable technology. One of the groups he's preparing to speak for as we write this book is in the insurance industry. Many agents in the insurance business are concerned about the use of portable technology and how to best deploy this in the real world.

A way to get more attention in that industry would be to start with the question, "Are you struggling to use portable technology and wanting to write more business?" Another title could be, "Discover how the latest smartphones and tablets can help you to write more business and be a top producer."

Notice that we are using key terms that are known and used by the insurance industry. Terry has done his research to understand problems that insurance agents are confronting today. Make it your goal to continually increase your knowledge of key terms, problem areas, and solutions that are unique to your audience. Be a resource that your audience can't find elsewhere, and they will want to engage with you and your content more.

Tip 8: Engage and Nurture Your Community

You must engage with your community, being there for them and answering their questions. The really successful social media ninjas will go beyond mere engagement. They discover what community members sincerely want to know about, and they don't engage in those areas that are considered superfluous or unnecessary by the community.

For instance, few people would find it valuable to know that you had a pizza for lunch. Many in business would find this information superfluous. However, if people in your city are looking for a good place for lunch today and you send a quick message that they are having a sale on pizza at Terry's Pizza Shop at the corner of Fourth and Main from 11 until 2 today, you will get attention. That information would be relevant to those in your town who are looking for a place for lunch and who like pizza. By creating messages that are relevant to your audience, you get more attention and more followers.

As you engage, you want to nurture. Help community members along and help others to build their business as well. In business we are all trying to increase sales and be more productive. If you could help nurture people along the path and give them genuine helpful assistance, they will remember this. This is the attitude of helping others and contributing and giving—it always matters most.

Tip 9: Stay Connected

It's one thing to connect with people. It is another thing to engage people. The best social ninjas are those who find meaningful ways to stay connected with important people. Discover what areas you can help them with on a regular basis. This means knowing the person and the needs that person has at any given moment.

For instance, if you know of a fellow thought leader who is working on a book that is coming out soon, any information you can contribute along that line would be helpful and would be appreciated. Even more important would be to help a fellow thought leader to market and sell more copies of his or her book. This has to be handled in a delicate and professional way. You don't want to sour your relationship with your own followers by constantly promoting someone else's material. Think about win-win-win situations. Think about how you can create a situation that is a win for your followers who are reading your material as well as your colleague you want to promote, and of course, yourself. Telling your followers about a genuinely good source of learning can be helpful. If you have a colleague who is putting on a very informative webinar, it can be extraordinarily helpful for your market to tell them about it.

These are all good ways to stay connected to your market. Stay current with what is important in the world today and particularly those areas that are important to your community.

Use tools like Google Alerts to stay up on hot topics as they happen. Google Alerts notifies you when a particular topic or phrase is used somewhere on the net. If you are trying to help a particular individual, make sure that you set up a Google Alert with the person's name and topics that are important to him or her. This way you would be able to alert people of a news release, or a mention about them somewhere on the net. This builds goodwill and helps you to be seen as a vital person to know. How can this help you with your Klout Score? By itself, it will not help you. However, if you take action on that information and connect with others in a creative, relevant way, it is highly probable they will respond. You are being alerted to new, current information. When you take action on that, you'll be more of a good social media citizen and you'll be engaging with others.

Tip 10: Become the "Go To" Person in Your Community

The time, money, and effort you expend to achieve this goal will pay rich dividends for you in building your business—and enhancing your Klout Score.

A marketing guru in Australia, Winston Marsh, shared with us recently how he had a seminar that was taught by technology expert Gihan Perera, who advocated this position. Gihan was speaking to a group of dentists and encouraged them to be the "go to" dentist in their community.[1]

This is the philosophy we shared earlier in Chapter 8. Dr. Tom Stanley, coauthor of the book *The Millionaire Next Door*, advocates this. You want to position yourself as the "go to" person in your community. In the physical world, this would mean that you know about good dentists on the north side of town or Realtors on the west side of town. People would see you as the person to know for references, and they would want to be in your good graces so that you would recommend them.

The same principle applies in the digital world and particularly with social media. You want to be seen as *the* resource that everyone wants to know. Even more, you want to be seen as the resource that other people want recommending them. If you do this in the digital world, your influence will increase dramatically.

This is a position that must be earned. It does not come about instantly. It will take time and practice, and you will learn through trial and error. Yes, you will make some mistakes. Hey, you are a human being! If you make mistakes, look at them as a learning experience to keep you moving toward your goal.

Tip 11: Feed Your Beast

This phrase comes from Robert Scoble. Writing a blog or doing a podcast requires a lot of effort. Many people can get started with it, but they lose steam after a while and their podcast goes dry. Scoble talks about this task as his "beast." He said, "I have a beast to feed and need to work on every morning. I have to find something to feed it. Otherwise what separates me from every other person?"[2]

This is the task that all thought leaders have when producing content in today's ever-hungry digital world. You need to come up with ideas that are going to be worth the time and attention that your readers will pay to consume what you have produced.

In the same interview where Robert Scoble talked about his beast, Mitch Joel, a well-known podcaster and blogger, talked about having a "Nose for News." He went on to describe this as the constant awareness and curiosity to look for stories that will be relevant for your community.[3]

That is what you will do as a thought leader. Realize that you need to "feed your beast" every day. In order to do that effectively, always keep your eyes and ears open for stories that would be of interest to your community.

We like the way that Australian marketing guru Winston Marsh says it as he describes himself as an "information vacuum cleaner." By this he means he is constantly looking for information and gathering useful ideas that he can repurpose and amplify to help his community.

Tip 12: Become a Storyteller

Throughout history and across all cultures, people have known the value of being able to tell a compelling story. As it was true centuries ago in jungles when tribespeople would gather around the local storyteller and listen with enchantment and engagement, it's true in our frenetic world today. We love to hear stories. Use this human need to communicate your message.

Always be on the lookout for new stories and new ways that you can make your points. You will increase your readership and follower base as you have regular stories that people find compelling and that fall into the category of "must-read."

Tip 13: Share Others' Ideas

One of the most attractive things you can do as a thought leader to bring others into your community is to share valuable information that you have seen elsewhere. Always be on the lookout for good content. When you share this you help in three ways: (1) you help your community as they learn about new information that they would not have seen otherwise, (2) you help the people who you are referencing as you increase their community by introducing your community to them, (3) you help yourself as you are seen as the curator who knows what is good information. By sharing these ideas with others you increase your status in the community, your influence, and ultimately your Klout Score.

There is an app called Flipboard that is popular for the aggregation of material and sources of info that users desire. With this tool, the user can assemble various magazines, blogs, and other online sources of news, learning, entertainment, and more. This is important for thought leaders to be a source that aggregates great content. Be that source of aggregation—not aggravation!—for the user.

Tip 14: Be Fast in a Niche Market

There's an old saying that says, "Money loves speed." It is as true today as it has been for years. If you have a means of connecting with a vibrant community that is passionate about a particular cause or concept, you can make a major difference. If you become known as the "go to" person for new and breaking ideas, you will develop a large following. You want to be seen as the place to go when a news item breaks.

For instance, if you have a group of people who are passionate about a particular technology, then you want to be the place where people go to learn about that. As an example, Gizmodo.com is a website known for previewing new technology when it comes out.

Another example of a website like this is CNET.com. When Apple announces a new product line, many people flock to these sites and others to learn what is going on, what is the latest, and what they should do. These sites are excellent places for determining what is valid and what is real.

Long ago many people realized that the advertisements from many companies are not to be trusted. Of course they are biased. Of course they are trying to sell their products. Today many buyers put more respect in public relations and announcements than they do in advertising.

Remember that you don't find your big fans, they find you. If you try to "push" your activities onto them, you'll meet with natural resistance. Instead, do your research and find out what people are looking for today. Provide content so that your work goes viral and appeals to a wide range of people as they share what you're doing with their friends.

Tip 15: Always Provide Value First

It is important to always provide value first, even when promoting yourself. This is a critical marketing concept. You want to always provide value to others and give them a reason to pay attention to you. Remember that in today's world, attention is one of the most costly things that people can give you. When you ask people to do something for you or you're talking about a new promotion for yourself, be sure to provide them with value.

We know that Klout works with companies who will give perks to people in given markets who have high influential scores. Here's a ninja marketing trick you can use to build your own fan base. Much like companies are giving perks to those with high influential factors, you can give perks to those who are most influential and following you and interacting with you. For example, you could offer a special report or special video or special audio interview that solves a unique industry problem for a tightly knit market. You would offer this perk only for those who perform certain tasks.

These tasks might be asking them to complete a survey, call a number and leave their opinion on a given topic, or take some other action on your behalf that costs little of their time and effort but gives you great value. Many podcasts are now offering the bonus of simply broadcasting your message on their podcast if you leave a voice message through their website.

Let your imagination run on this one. Think of what your niche market will value. Is it an interview with a noted authority in that field? Could it be an instructional how-to video on a new gadget that is important to that market? Could it be an article with your predictions for a hot trend in that industry? Think of what is going to be very valuable to your market and costs you very little in cash that you can offer.

Imagine the value you can get by collecting survey results from top influencers in your given niche. The feedback they give you will be the raw material for your next content creation. If you are wondering what to write that is going to be compelling content for your next blog, find it out from the real surveys. A tool like Survey Monkey (www.surveymonkey.com) can help here. Tools like Speak Pipe (www.speakpipe.com) can help as well. Speak Pipe gives you the ability to allow visitors to your site to leave a recorded voice message. Other resources and how you can use them are referenced in the appendixes of this book.

Another example of how you can provide benefit to your fan base is through Google+ Hangouts. This is a tool that gives you the ability to have videoconferencing with up to 10 people. You can broadcast to the world through your YouTube channel if you'd like. One value that you can offer as a thought leader to some select fans would be to have "lunch" over a Google+ Hangout for an exclusive group of people who were the first to opt in for a new report. You could make an offer for a new product and invite the first five people to an exclusive meeting. In this Google+ Hangout, you can reveal new secrets about something of value to that industry.

Always think about how you can leverage technology in order to help people more. Doing a Hangout on Google+ would not cost you any cash—only time and effort. It would be of great value to some select fans to be able to follow you and interact with you directly through that Google+ Hangout.

If you can position yourself as the thought leader in a particular niche who releases new information the fastest, you will build a strong following. As we like to say: you will then build a strong following, it will grow your business—and you will raise your Klout Score.

Tip 16: Have Fun!

Human beings love to have fun. When you can create an environment for a special niche where people learn valuable information and have a lot of fun, you are going to build a follower base. Leverage tools and technology like Google+ Hangouts and Skype video where you can have a fun, information-rich environment. If you can make promotional events fun and highly desirable, it is only natural that you will attract more people.

Using the fun principle is even more important when you're promoting a new product or service. Sure you can promote something without blending in a lot of fun, but in today's world many people mix social and business. That means you want to have fun baked into the mix from the beginning.

How do you determine what's fun? Don't rely only on what you consider fun. Ask a lot of questions and find out from your target market what they consider fun. Then build that fun around accomplishing a new objective like a product launch, a webinar, or other activity.

Tip 17: Be Consistent

In doing our research for this book, we made a personal visit to Klout headquarters in San Francisco. One of the interviews that we had was with Joe Fernandez, the cofounder and CEO of Klout. When we asked Joe what he would recommend for people to raise their Klout Score, we heard something very interesting.

Joe said that it was most important to be consistent with your social media efforts. Some people have suggested spending an hour or two hours a day on social media. Joe says that he regularly spends time on social media throughout the day. He went on to say, "The net has a very short attention span. If you're not in the cadence of the conversation your effectiveness is dampened. Make it a part of your routine to do something 10 or so times a day. One every hour on Twitter is not too much."[4]

This is most interesting. The man who is the CEO of Klout and who came up with the original idea says it is most important to regularly be on social media providing valuable information on a consistent basis.

What you do not want to do is to send out one tweet every other month. This will not help your Klout Score increase!

While working with social media throughout the day works for him, Joe recommends that each person find the comfort style that works for him or her. Many people are not able to connect with Twitter or Facebook 10 times a day. Find the rhythm and the cadence that works for you and your lifestyle and your job requirements.

Economist Mary Kelly, PhD, uses social media extensively and offered these two points related to consistency in your messaging:

1. Enjoy social networks. If social networking becomes a chore, either change your routine or change your mindset. Social networking should be an enjoyable way to get to know other people on multiple levels.
2. Check in to your favorite social network every day. Consistency is key. Pick one or two social media avenues and consistently post, blog, or comment.[5]

Tip 18: Use Social Media for Communication

If you have a message you need to send to someone, rather than sending it through e-mail, consider using Facebook or Twitter. You don't improve your Klout Score with a private message on Facebook or a direct message on Twitter. However, if you have more public (important!) communication on either of these, your Klout Score will be affected positively. Therefore, a good strategy is to request public comments and suggestions to be directed to you on Facebook or Twitter as public messages. Make it a point to respond to these in a timely manner so more of your audience can see and react.

The amount of e-mail you receive has no effect on your Klout Score. You can boost your Klout Score by asking for people to contact you via Twitter. If you receive more communication through Twitter, you are likely to have a higher Klout Score as others are mentioning you and connecting with you through that medium.

Think of creative ways to encourage people to respond to you through Facebook and Twitter. This will be a preferred form of communication to increase your Klout Score. Just remember that these messages are public, so don't put anything on Twitter or Facebook that you don't want the world to see!

Tip 19: Squeeze Social Media Connecting Time into "Scrap Time" Blocks

Let's face it, we are all time-starved and pressed to use every available moment to the best we can. In today's busy lifestyle, it is hard to get things done, let alone try to take on a task like social media. The mere thought of engaging on several platforms with people around the world can seem daunting, if not downright impossible.

Yet many people are successfully engaging in social media when they have the right system. Having the right system that helps you to get what needs to be done accomplished is worth discovering and perfecting.

It sometimes means that you'll do some work with Twitter or Facebook when you have some "scrap time" available. Alan Stevens is a UK-based media coach, PR expert, and professional speaker. He gave us an excellent suggestion on how he finds that "scrap time" in his busy schedule and manages to connect with people through social media:

Whenever I have some downtime in a cafe or waiting for a plane, I set up a Twitter clinic. I post a message asking for questions on my area of expertise, using a hashtag such as #prclinic. I answer every question that is sent. This serves several purposes. Firstly, it helps people, which is most important. Secondly, it allows people to see me demonstrating my expertise in public, which helps to raise my profile. Thirdly, I keep all of the questions by favoriting them, which allows me to see what the hot topics are, and to tailor my tweets, speeches and articles accordingly.[6]

Tip 20: Remember, It Is Not Just About Boosting Your Klout Score

If you've made it this far in the book, you know being successful today in social media is not just trying to boost your Klout Score. One of the people we had a chance to visit at Klout headquarters was Sahana Ullagaddi, Community Manager at Klout, who said it very well: "It's great if you have a very high Klout Score, but what are you doing with it?"[7]

If you're in business, you need more than just a high Klout Score. You need to earn money! We have often talked among ourselves about certain people we know who have a high Klout Score but are not doing very well in business. There's nothing wrong with that if that is the lifestyle that they choose. However, for those of us who have bills to pay, the Klout Score must directly relate to the business bottom line.

Your success should not be about aiming for a high Klout Score. Instead, make it your goal to consistently provide value and help others to solve their problems, using the right protocols of social media. If you regularly practice good social media behavior, you will do well in business. As you do well in business, the natural effect will be for your Klout Score to increase.

Figure 10.1 illustrates what you need to do to be effective in social media. We like to call it the ninja-level social media effectiveness guide. It takes all three components of this triangle to be truly effective at a ninja level.

It starts with engagement. This will include first of all listening to what your audience is saying. It also involves watching and paying attention to what their areas of interest happen to be. Don't make the mistake of assuming that you know what they are looking for.

Notice on this diagram that it starts with your engagement, as we have said often in this book. Proceed from there to create content

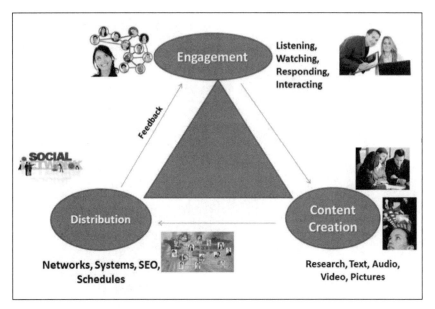

Figure 10.1 Ninja-level social media effectiveness

based on your research and what you've heard from others. Finally, you find the platforms and means of distributing your content.

The most important part of this graph is the arrows that show these are connected to each other and they constantly link to other areas. Note that after you have gone through distribution it goes back to engagement, where you get feedback on what others are saying regarding the material you have disseminated. Yes, social media effectiveness is an ongoing and never-ending activity. And that just makes it more fun!

CHAPTER 11

Getting Started with Klout

The secret of getting ahead is getting started.
—MARK TWAIN

Signing up for Klout is a very easy, streamlined process.

Step 1: Choose Twitter or Facebook

Start by choosing whether you want to connect your Klout account to your Twitter profile or your Facebook profile. See Figure 11.1.

Figure 11.1 Choose Twitter or Facebook

Step 2: Choose Topics You're Knowledgable About

Klout will give you a list of topics its information indicates you may be an expert on. Enter topics that you like to talk about and that you want to be known for. See Figure 11.2.

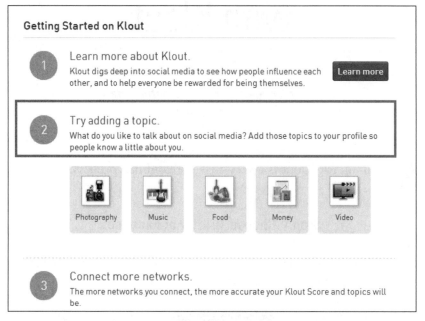

Figure 11.2 Choose topics

Step 3: Connect Your Accounts

If you have more social media accounts, you can connect them in this step. Just click "Connect" next to each account you want to connect, then click "Continue" once you're finished. See Figure 11.3.

A question we are often asked is, "Should I connect my Personal Facebook Profile or my Facebook Page?" For most people, connecting the Personal Facebook Profile will yield a higher score than the Page due to Facebook's algorithm.

Another question we are often asked is, "Is it good to connect all my networks even if I am not active on them?" According to Klout

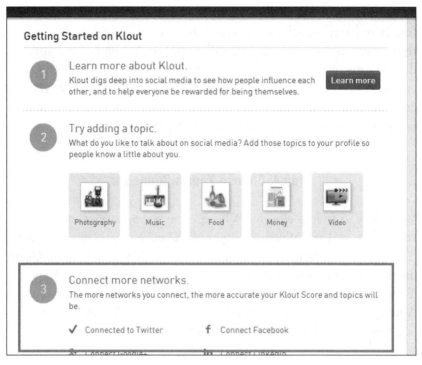

Figure 11.3 Connect accounts

CEO Joe Fernandez, the answer is yes: "Connecting your accounts never hurts you. It can only help you."[1]

Clean Your Klout Closet Regularly

Once a week, go to http://klout.com/#/manage-topics to adjust your topics. Note: This is something you want to check on regularly as Klout will assign topics to you that may or may not be relevant. For example, once Gina tweeted about a marketing campaign by Harley-Davidson that she really liked. A week later, "Harley-Davidson" showed up as a topic that Gina was influential about. Since Gina has never owned or ridden a Harley-Davidson (not yet!), she deleted that as one of her topics.

Gina calls this "cleaning your Klout closet": reviewing your topics once a week, deleting ones that don't work for you, and adding ones that do.

As there is not a way to say that you are an expert in a certain functional area—such as speaker, author, cyclist—it is wise to select these areas as "topics" you are influential in. While being a speaker does not mean that you are an expert in the business of speaking, it is currently one of the ways that you can let the world know that you are an expert speaker. Speakers might also include choosing conferences, keynotes, and meetings as one of their topics.

Step 4: Choose Your Influencers

Who do you follow closely? Who do you see as an authority? Who would you call an influencer of yours? Klout will present you with a list of people. Again, select from the list by clicking on them. Go to http://klout.com/#/username/influencers to choose your influencers. This is another area that you should check and change occasionally. Adding people to your influencer list will often inspire someone to add you as one of their influencers. This adds Klout juice.

Step 5: Changing Your Description

Your description appears directly under your name, picture, and Klout Score in your profile. When you sign up for your account, Klout

Figure 11.4 Gina's Klout profile

will ask you if you want to use your Twitter description or provide your own. We recommend making one specific to Klout. Be sure to include topics you want to be known for. It is even okay to state what you would like to receive +Ks for. See Figures 11.4 and 11.5.

Figure 11.5 Terry's Klout profile

To change your description, go to "Settings" in the upper right corner, then fill out the "About" field. See Figure 11.6.

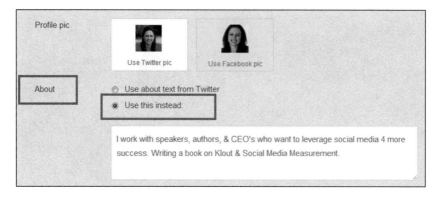

Figure 11.6 Filling out the "About" field

That's all there is to it! Your Klout profile is set up and ready to go. You've got your accounts, your topics, your influencers, and your profile all set up.

In the following chapters, we will consider some of the major networks that contribute to your Klout Score: Twitter, Facebook, LinkedIn, Wikipedia, Instagram, and others.

The bigger the network, the more likely it is to factor into your score. Check with experts in these networks to learn about the best ways to engage. Many of the tips we provide will work in all social networks. Please reference Klout's website to get the latest information about what is counting toward your Klout Score.[2]

CHAPTER 12

Using Twitter to Raise Your Klout Score

I read Twitter all the time, even though I rarely tweet.
—WILL.I.AM OF THE BLACK EYED PEAS

Twitter is a powerful network for sharing content, engaging with people, listening, and getting the word out about what you do. And since Twitter is one of the main drivers of your Klout Score, we have given special attention to ways you can improve your score. According to Kathryn Rose, author of *Solving the Social Media Puzzle* and cofounder of the Social Buzz Club: "In my opinion, Twitter is the main driver of conversations. Twitter does not have an "edgerank" algorithm so every tweet goes to every follower. It is a great way to connect, monitor, and interact with your core key audience and other influencers. Use Twitter lists and tools like Listorious (now part of Muck Rack) and Twellow to find and engage with key people."[1] (See Figure 12.1 for one of Kathryn Rose's tweets.)

Figure 12.1 Tweet by Kathryn Rose

WHAT KLOUT COUNTS ON TWITTER

Klout logo   **Twitter logo**

Klout currently places a lot of emphasis on these actions:

- Retweets: Retweets increase your influence by exposing your content to extended follower networks.
- Mentions: People seeking your attention by mentioning you is a strong signal of influence. We also take into account the differences in types of mentions, including "via" and "cc."
- List memberships: Being included on lists curated by other users demonstrates your areas of influence.
- Followers: Follower count is one factor in your Score, but we heavily favor engagement over size of audience.
- Replies: Replies show that you are consistently engaging your network with quality content.[2]

Here are some ideas about how to increase your engagement on Twitter.

Retweets

To get more retweets (RTs), make your tweets:

- **Short.** Tweets with 70 to 100 characters get retweeted the most (120 characters max).
- **Funny.** Humorous quotes get retweeted a lot.
- **Pithy.** Make your tweet meaty but concise.

- **Controversial.** Take a stance on a current event to stir up interaction.
- **Topical.** Add a humorous twist on a current event or trending topic.
- **Findable.** Include a hashtag so that your tweet will be seen by people who aren't following you but who are interested in a specific topic. For an example of a retweet, see Figure 12.2.

Figure 12.2 Retweet of two great tweeters: Miriam Slozberg @msmir and Carly Alyssa Thorne @CarlyAThorne by Gina. Notice the Klout Score by the name. This appears in Gina's Twitter stream because she uses a special Klout app for Twitter on Google Chrome.

EXPERT TIP

If you want to be retweeted, start by tweeting others. This will start you on the path to building relationships that you did not have previously as everyone loves to be retweeted.[3]

Hashtags

How do hashtags work and why are they so powerful?

Think of a hashtag as a virtual clubhouse on Twitter where people "gather" and discuss topics of mutual interest. For example, people interested in the economic theories of Friedrich Hayek might tweet with the hashtag #hayek (see Figure 12.3). In doing so, they are joining in a virtual conversation about this topic. They may agree or disagree. The point is that they are joining in the conversation.

Figure 12.3 #hashtags (Gina's Twitter page with #hayek)

To join in the conversation, all you need to do is type the hashtag of interest into the Twitter search bar. If you don't know what hashtag to use, just experiment. As you experiment, notice the hashtags that other people are using. Then, enter those hashtags into the search bar. A slightly more advanced way to enter the virtual clubhouse of discussion around a certain topic is to use tools like these:

- **TweetChat (www.tweetchat.com)** enables easy participation in the "chat room." TweetChat automatically applies the hashtag to your tweets and makes it super easy to follow people who are tweeting with your chosen hashtag.
- **Twubs (www.twubs.com)** allows you to "register" your hashtag and participate in the virtual discussion. Similar to TweetChat, Twubs automatically applies the hashtag to your tweets. (There is no real registration for hashtags. Anyone can use any hashtag they wish. Hashtags don't belong to anyone.)

Hashtag discussions can go on around the clock. Sometimes there are focused specific periods designated for twitter chats about a specific topic. Figure 12.4 shows a page for tweets about #WalkingDead on Twubs.com.

Figure 12.4 Twubs.com #WalkingDead

@ Mentions

Here are some ways to get more @ mentions.

1. Make It Easy for People to Mention Your Twitter Handle in a Post.

Use these blogging tools for WordPress to make it easy for people to tweet your content in a way that increases your influence (and thus increases your Klout Score). Be sure to fill in a good tweet with each post you do. Include your Twitter handle and make the title short.

Tweet Embed is a plug-in that puts a tweet right inside your blog post or page. See Figure 12.5.

Another plug-in called Tweet This makes it easy for readers to tweet your content. Figure 12.6 shows how Jay Baer used Tweet This in an interview he did with Matt Thomson, vice president of business development at Klout.[4]

Gina particularly likes the Click to Tweet plug-in by Todaymade because it is easy to use. See Figure 12.7.

Figure 12.5 Example of the Tweet Embed plug-in

Figure 12.6 Example of the Tweet This plug-in with Jay Baer
and Matt Thomson

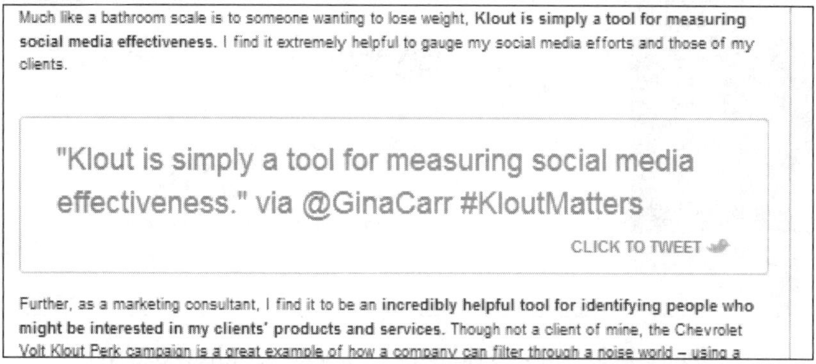

Much like a bathroom scale is to someone wanting to lose weight, Klout is simply a tool for measuring social media effectiveness. I find it extremely helpful to gauge my social media efforts and those of my clients.

"Klout is simply a tool for measuring social media effectiveness." via @GinaCarr #KloutMatters

CLICK TO TWEET

Further, as a marketing consultant, I find it to be an incredibly helpful tool for identifying people who might be interested in my clients' products and services. Though not a client of mine, the Chevrolet Volt Klout Perk campaign is a great example of how a company can filter through a noise world – using a

Figure 12.7 Example of the Click to Tweet plug-in by Todaymade

2. Create Tweets That Compliment Several People at Once.

Make your complimentary tweets 120 characters or less so they are easy to retweet. I use www.ifttt.com to automatically tweet "group tweets" like the one shown in Figure 12.8 every week.

Figure 12.8 Complimentary group tweet

3. Participate in Follow Friday Tweets (#FF).

Recommend some of your favorite tweeters to your tribe with a tweet like the one shown in Figure 12.9.

4. Tweet about Twitter.

Tweets about Twitter, like the one in Figure 12.10, tend to get a lot of retweets.

Figure 12.9 Follow Friday #FF tweets—Andrew Szabo

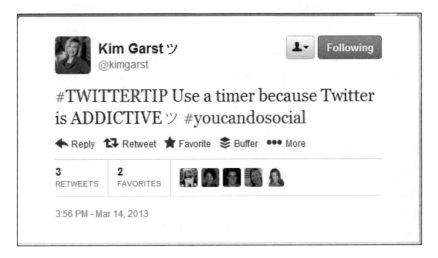

Figure 12.10 Tweet about Twitter by @KimGarst

Lists

With over 500 million Twitter users, Twitter can be a very noisy place. In addition to tools like HootSuite and TweetDeck, a Twitter list allows you to see what people on the list are tweeting about. It effectively allows you to set a tweet stream with just those people. It is, in short, a convenient way to see what is going on with people who are important to you.

An easy way to get on more Twitter lists is to participate in TweetChats. People who participate in these will often add fellow participants to a Twitter list. I agree with marketing expert Gina Schreck, who said, "I believe that finding and participating in TweetChats is one of the best networking and community building activities out there. You get to meet and chat with many people who are in your industry or focus area to begin building relationships."[5]

Followers

How do you get more followers? One of the ways is to follow more people yourself and to interact with them. Here is what social media guru Gina Schreck had to say:

> *A great tip for those new to Twitter and trying to build up their network is to first, follow smart people. Connect with quality people who are posting content that is interesting and helpful in your area of focus, and to increase the odds that they will follow back, you should read through their last 20–30 tweets and find something to either retweet or something you can reply to. This will begin the relationship and increase the odds that they will follow back.*[6]

EXPERT TIP

Twitter engagement will play a huge roll in increasing your Klout Score, so make sure that you reply to people when they tweet you. Thank people when they retweet your tweets and work on building relationships so that people will be more apt to share your content when you tweet it.[7]

Engage influencers in your niche. Klout rewards you for engaging with people who have higher Klout Scores than you do, so it is beneficial to reach out to influencers in a positive and authentic way. Respond to what they are tweeting or make a comment on their content. Be unique and stand out in some way so that you will grab their attention.[8]

See Kim Garst's fabulous Twitter profile and background in Figure 12.11.

Figure 12.11 Kim Garst Twitter profile

Tools

In summary, Twitter is a great tool to use to engage with and connect with important people. If you're getting started with it, get an account and plan to follow people who are important to you and your industry. Plan to spend some time there to get to know the protocols and proper communication responses to be a good social media citizen.

Klout originally used only Twitter for its social media monitoring. Even today, Twitter use is a big factor in determining one's Klout Score. Most everyone who has a higher Klout Score makes use of Twitter, at least in some capacity.

Think of Twitter as a great listening tool to find out what is going on in your market and your industry. You can search for key phrases that people are looking for and searching. As you practice with it, and build a following, you'll find that it can help you engage more and build your digital influence. Doing all of those activities in the right way will help raise your Klout Score.

CHAPTER 13

Using Facebook to Raise Your Klout Score

I really believe that when you give people authentic identity, which is what Facebook does, and you can be your real self and connect with real people online, things will change.
—SHERYL SANDBERG, COO OF FACEBOOK

With over 1 billion users, Facebook is the 800-pound gorilla in the social media room (as of this writing). Facebook has huge potential for increasing engagement with your fan base, engaging with customers, and raising your Klout Score for the social media–savvy thought leader. In this chapter, we will show you some examples of what you can do to better engage and take advantage of Facebook's possibilities to boost your Klout Score.

Facebook's functionality makes it easy for people to interact with one another. That is one of its biggest draws. People love to see where their friends hang out, what they're doing, and what they think about various topics.

Facebook Interactions That Affect Your Klout Score

Here are the interactions that contribute most to your Klout Score on Facebook:

- **Mentions.** When you are tagged in a post in Facebook. An example would be "Hello Terry Brock (tagged). Hope you are having a good day there in Orlando." If that message was sent

to Terry Brock (using his Facebook tag), it provides a Klout
signal that can positively affect Terry Brock's Klout Score.

- **Tags**. When you are tagged in a photo in Facebook. This also
  provides a positive Klout signal. For instance, if you see a
  picture with Gina Carr, and you're a friend of hers, you can
  click on it, then hover over her picture. When Facebook asks
  to type a name, you'd type "Gina Carr," and she would be
  tagged. She would also be notified that you had tagged her in
  a photo.
- **Likes**. When people click "Like" on something you post or
  share. Think of this as a "wave to a friend across a noisy restaurant." It is not a huge commitment in the digital world, but
  all the "Likes" you get are a positive influence to build your
  Klout Score.
- **Comments**. When people comment on something you have
  posted. This is a biggy! By leaving a comment, you let
  people know what you think. Any comment that is left on
  your page by others produces a positive signal for your
  Klout Score.
- **Wall posts**. When others post on your wall.

Currently, Klout only counts *either* your Facebook Personal Profile
or your Facebook Page, not both. For most non-celebrity individuals, the Facebook Personal Profile will yield better results than the
Facebook Page.

Group interactions are not important to your Klout Score.
Although groups are great places to collaborate about social sharing
and to discuss important issues, the actual activity that takes place
in Facebook groups—even public groups—counts very little toward
your Klout Score.

Tips on Facebook Activities to
Raise Your Klout Score

Here are some ideas about how to increase interactions on Facebook
that count toward your Klout Score.

1. Ask a Simple Fill-in-the-Blank Question.

Keep in mind that people on Facebook are always in a hurry. They don't want to spend a lot of time on a single post. Make it easy for them by asking a simple question like the one shown in Figure 13.1.

Figure 13.1 Blue collar comedy tour Facebook engagement question

2. Post Your Advice, Philosophy, or Thoughts About Life.

Marketing genius Randy Gage generates a ton of engagement with his daily suggestions about how to become more prosperous and successful (Figure 13.2).

3. Post About Your Interests.

Posts about pets, gardens, coffee, and such generate a lot of tweets. Take a look at the post in Figure 13.3 from Australia's business marketing guru Winston Marsh.

Figure 13.2 Randy Gage fan page engagement on Facebook

Figure 13.3 Winston Marsh's office mates—dogs and cats at bookcase

4. Post About Life.

Social media marketing genius Laura Rubinstein shares a little of her life in the post shown in Figure 13.4.

Figure 13.4 Laura Rubinstein shares a little of her life on Facebook

5. Post About What You Are Thinking or Learning or Doing.

We love the post by Facebook expert Andrea Vahl (Figure 13.5) where she is having some fun . . . and sharing that she was doing something really cool (filming at Icosa).

Andrea had this to say about Facebook posts:

To increase your engagement on your Facebook Page, post a variety of types of posts (links, text-only, and photos) because each one can get different reach in the News Feed but also elicit different response from your audience. Ask questions to get conversation started. Also post fun and social posts (cartoons, funny videos, etc.) from time to time because people are on Facebook to be social, not always to talk about your business niche.[1]

Figure 13.5 Andrea giving the weather report from Icosa

6. Post Something Funny.

The picture shown in Figure 13.6 was posted by Gina Schreck as her Facebook cover picture. Gina is the author of a book about Twitter and is quite a Twitter genius.

7. Write an Informative Post.

Business communications expert Dianna Booher does a great job of sharing a little communication lesson with a simple post from a personal experience (Figure 13.7).

Figure 13.6 Twitter bird cartoon

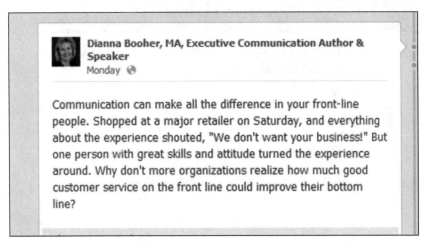

Figure 13.7 Dianna Booher's informative
Facebook post on communication skills

8. Post Something Inspiring.

Inspirational posts often get a lot of Klout juice because people like
to share these. Edel O'Mahony does a beautiful job with her inspirational posts like the one in Figure 13.8.

Figure 13.8 Edel O'Mahony's inspirational Facebook post.
Edel smartly included her website in small, subtle text.

Figure 13.9 Kim Garst demonstrates a Facebook post
with a clear call to action

9. Include a Call to Action.

If you want people to like your post or take a specific action, ask them to with a call to action (CTA). Figure 13.9 shows an example from Kim Garst.

10. Share Something Thought Provoking.

Figure 13.10 shows a terrific simple post presented in a clever way by sales wiz Jane Garee.

Figure 13.10 A creative, thought-provoking statement by Jane Garee

11. Compliment Someone.

Figure 13.11 is a great example of *Wall Street Journal* bestselling author Bob Burg telling his tribe about his friend's new book.

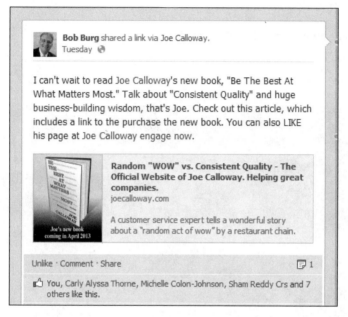

Figure 13.11 Bob Burg introduces Joe Calloway's book with a compliment

12. Post on a Current Event.

Tie your post to your area of expertise if possible. Figure 13.12 is a great example by Jeffrey Hayzlett, leadership and marketing expert.

Figure 13.12 Jeffrey Hayzlett's post on a current event

EXPERT TIP

On your Facebook personal profile, be sure to allow Followers so you can expand the reach of your publicly shared posts to a wider audience. (Follow simply means that anyone on Facebook can subscribe to receive your public posts in their news feed—not unlike the way Twitter works.) Facebook expert Mari Smith suggests, "Along with some personal content, periodically provide informative content pertaining to your area of expertise that is easily shareable, ideally that includes an image, and includes a call to action to share the post."[2] See her example in Figure 13.13.

Figure 13.13 Mari Smith post about Mark Zuckerberg

Many people say that posting pictures tends to draw more attention, hence giving you more likes and comments. In our experience, we have found the pictures do tend to attract a lot more likes and comments, thus creating a higher Klout Score. However, lately we have heard from others, and have experienced ourselves, that a well-crafted text-only message can also draw a lot of likes and comments. It depends on what is said in the target market. It also depends upon Facebook's EdgeRank, which changes.

We recommend that you test what works for you. Keep records of what you have done (e.g., "Picture of my friend Bob," posting a picture of a scene at the lake, text message about success, etc.). Then note how many comments and likes you get on those particular activities. Your actual results *will* vary. What works for one person, might not work as well for another. You need to track your own progress and results.

Fortunately, Klout Moments helps you identify which posts and pictures received the most engagement. This is one of the reasons it is important to visit Klout daily to see what is getting the most activity (Figure 13.14).

Have fun working with Facebook! It is a great tool for connecting and engaging with people. As we have been saying throughout this

Figure 13.14 Klout said that this picture of Gina, Scott Friedman, and Terry at the National Speakers Association of Colorado meeting was one of Gina's most popular posts

book, engagement is what social media is all about. Facebook is an important tool for you to use for engaging with those people who are important to you.

If you receive likes, shares, and comments on the content you create, that indicates that your content has sparked engagement. If you receive mentions, that is an indicator that others are engaging with you and that also contributes to your score. The number of friends and subscribers have some bearing on your score but is somewhat insignificant. If you do not interact with them, the numbers do little good.[3]
—MIRIAM SLOZBERG

CHAPTER 14

Using LinkedIn to Raise Your Klout Score

Social networks do best when they tap into one of the seven deadly sins. Facebook is ego. Zynga is sloth. LinkedIn is greed.
—REID HOFFMAN, COFOUNDER OF LINKEDIN

L inkedIn is one of the most powerful networks for creating business connections. Unlike the more "social" networks like Facebook and Twitter, LinkedIn is much more business oriented. You don't see people posting pictures of their dogs or what they had for lunch on LinkedIn. Much like the formal office environment, things are a bit more "official" in the land of LinkedIn.

Although LinkedIn is arguably very important for business, because of its less interactive nature, LinkedIn does not account for a significant part of your Klout Score.

Bottom line: if you want a high Klout Score, spend more time on Twitter, Facebook, or Google+. If you want a bigger bank account, spend more time on LinkedIn.

What Klout Counts on LinkedIn

Klout currently factors in these signals from LinkedIn:[1]

- **Title**. Your reported title on LinkedIn is a signal of your real-world influence and is persistent.
- **Connections**. Your connection graph helps validate your real-world influence.

- **Recommenders.** The recommenders in your network add additional signals to the contribution LinkedIn makes to your Klout Score.
- **Comments.** As a reaction to content you share, comments also reflect direct engagement by your network.[2]

How to Increase Your Engagement on LinkedIn

Here are some ideas about how to increase your engagement on LinkedIn. The most important thing you must do in LinkedIn is to have a professional, succinct, error-free profile.

Make sure that your title is reflected in your work experience. Here are some great examples. Jeffrey Hayzlett is going to pick up a lot of Klout juice because his profile reflects his CEO and CMO titles (Figure 14.1). It also associates him with a large company, Eastman Kodak, of which he was the CMO.

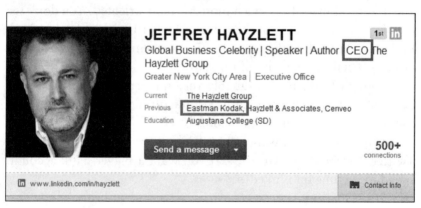

Figure 14.1 Jeff Hayzlett's LinkedIn profile

We love the way that Viveka von Rosen has used the prime real estate in her contact info section to offer a summary instead of her address (Figure 14.2).

Viveka also makes it easy for people to review her summary (Figure 14.3).

Add Rich Media to your LinkedIn profile. LinkedIn now allows you to add videos, web pages, pictures, and other media to your

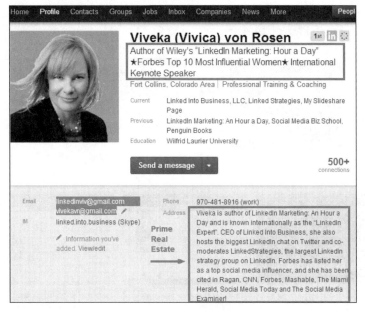

Figure 14.2 Viveka von Rosen's LinkedIn profile

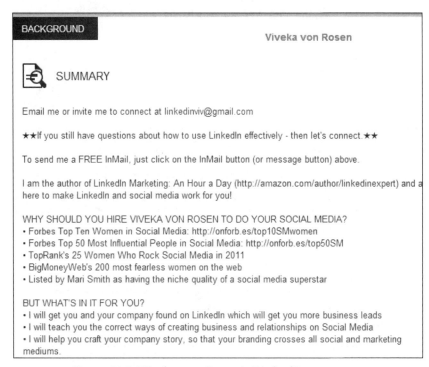

Figure 14.3 Viveka von Rosen's LinkedIn summary

LinkedIn profile. Take a look at how Viveka von Rosen has done that on hers (Figure 14.4).

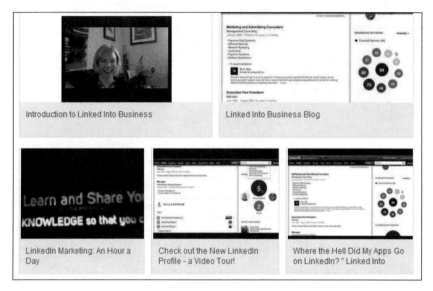

Figure 14.4 Viveka von Rosen's videos

Figure 14.5 Jeff Hayzlett's titles

Jeff Hayzlett's LinkedIn profile includes his role as the chief marketing officer and vice president of Kodak (Figure 14.5). His profile, combined with Kodak's' company profile on LinkedIn, adds significantly to Jeff's real-world influence component. Jeff's recommendations also contribute to the LinkedIn component of his Klout Score.

The education section plays a role in establishing your real-world credentials on LinkedIn (Figure 14.6) and counts toward your offline influence on Klout. Be sure to post accurate information here.

 EDUCATION

Gina Carr

Harvard Business School
MBA, Entrepreneurship, Marketing
1988 – 1990

Activities and Societies: President, Southeastern Club Active in Real Estate, Entrepreneurship, and Adventure Clubs

Georgia Institute of Technology
BIE, Industrial Engineering
1978 – 1984

Activities and Societies: President, Omicron Delta Kappa National Leadership Honor Society Winner, Georgette P. Burdell Award, Society of Women Engineers Water Ski Club, President Student Government Representative

Figure 14.6 Gina Carr's education section on LinkedIn

Make sure that your company has its own listing on LinkedIn. This is important for establishing your offline or real-world influence as part of your Klout Score.

EXPERT TIP

I am addicted to CardMunch App. After a speaking engagement, I gather the cards together, take a quick shot with my camera, and add them to CardMunch. I can instantly connect with the people I just met, put a face to a name, and they feel immediately acknowledged by me. Having real, personable relationships is essential to me on social networks. This enables me to connect fast.[3]

I love Klout as it is a great barometer for my social media contribution. I work very hard at content creation, and I want to make sure my impact is making a difference and being broadcasted in a way that makes an impact. My Klout Score keeps me in check.
—**HEATHER LUTZE**

CHAPTER 15

Using Other Networks to Raise Your Klout Score

Anyone who thinks new technology isn't going to keep changing the world has got their head in the sand.
—SIR RICHARD BRANSON

As of this writing, Twitter and Facebook are the major networks that affect your Klout Score. However, networks are constantly being added. In this chapter, we take a look at a few that should be on your Klout radar.

Wikipedia

With the Maxwell algorithm change in August 2012, Klout added Wikipedia as a way to determine offline influence.[1] Adding a Wikipedia page generally adds a nice boost in points to a Klout Score. We've seen five to fifteen points added when Klout adds a Wikipedia page to a profile.

If you already have a Wikipedia page, you need to ask Klout to include this for you. At the current time, the best way is to send a request to help@kloutsupport.com that includes the link to the Wikipedia page.

If you do not have a Wikipedia page, all we can say is good luck getting one. It is pretty tough. Because the editors at Wikipedia are focused on keeping the service unbiased and objective, they do not encourage you to pay someone to write an article about you. Current guidelines also prevent you from writing an article about yourself. And it is pretty difficult to write an article that meets their standards and adheres to their formatting, so you can't just get a friend to do it for you.

Therefore, the chances are slim that someone who understands the Wikipedia system—one of its editors—will write about you unless you are a well-known author, speaker, or celebrity. In Wiki-speak, you have to be "noteworthy." Literally, that means that you have been "written up" in reputable publications—online and offline.

However, if you do meet Wikipedia's requirement that you are notable enough for publication, you might get someone on your staff or in a public relations role to submit a page—with full disclosure of the relationship. If the page meets the other Wikipedia guidelines, it might be approved (see http://en.wikipedia.org/wiki/Wikipedia:Notability).

If you do get a Wikipedia page, Klout will be looking at a number of factors to determine how important the page is and thus how influential you are. Here are some of the factors considered:

- Inlinks. Measures the total number of inbound links to a page.
- Ratio of Inlinks to Outlinks. Compares the number of inbound links to a page to the number of outbound links.
- Page Importance (as measured by PageRank). Measured by applying a PageRank algorithm against the Wikipedia page graph.[2]

If you'd like to take a quick quiz to see if you meet the notability standards of Wikipedia, visit http://KloutMatters.com/wikipedia.

EXPERT TIP

When you think of Wikipedia, think of good ole' Honest Abe and his line, "government of the people, by the people, for the people." Wikipedia was established to be a resource "of the people, by the people, for the people." And when you, the individual, start trying to manipulate entries about yourself (or having someone else do it on your behalf), eventually you will be discovered. Their editorial guidelines and approval policies are strictly regulated.—Dianna Booher.[3]

Figure 15.1 Dianna Booher's profile featuring the Wikipedia page connection.

Bing

In an effort to further integrate an off-line component of influence, Klout is now counting the number of times a user is searched for on Bing. In order for this to affect your Klout Score, you must add Bing in your "settings" on Klout and "tag" articles on Bing that reference you. See Figure 15.2 for an example of a search on Bing.

Figure 15.2 Chris Brogan's high Klout Score is due
in part to searches on Bing

Klout Experts

Another way that Bing is affecting Klout is through "Klout Experts."
Klout Experts' answers to questions are being integrated into the Bing
search results with what appears to be a great deal of authority. This
is a new feature and is evolving.

"With Klout Experts, our goal is to enable every person to share
their passions and expertise with the world. Klout Experts will create a path to not only increasing your Klout Score, but also to helping others by sharing your insights and opinions."[4] —Joe Fernandez,
CEO and cofounder of Klout

Instagram

Klout recently integrated Instagram photos into the Klout Score. This
network is contributing powerfully to user scores. There are three important tips we can share about increasing your score with Instagram:

1. Use it. Instead of using other apps for taking photos, remember to use Instagram and to then share directly to Facebook,
   Twitter, and any other network counted by Klout.
2. Use hashtags. These allow your pictures and videos to be
   found and shared more easily.
3. Connect with friends. Actively review your Instragram account and link with your friends. Like and comment on their
   photos and they are likely to return the favor.

New York Times bestselling author Joel Comm had this to say
about Instagram:

A little goes a long way when using Instagram. Since Klout is deriving 10% of my network value to Instagram, I can post a photo and share it via Facebook, Twitter, Tumblr, Flickr and Foursquare. That share then trickles down to affect a number of sites all at once. Since I love sharing photos anyway, it makes sense to prioritize Instagram for sharing and engaging.[5]

See Figure 15.3 for more information about Instagram.

Figure 15.3 Gina Schreck's Getting Geeky fan page asks about Instagram.

Google+

As Google+ becomes more powerful and popular, it will factor more heavily into the Klout Score. As Google+ is very important for Google search, it is a network that needs to be part of your social media marketing strategy.

Amanda Blain is a Google+ expert. She explains: "Google+ is a true social 'give and take' network. You will likely be interacting with strangers based on common interests. Just like you would try to make a friend in real life, you need to talk about the other person (com-ment and interact on their posts), see them often (do this more than one time), and try to connect (hangout, mention, share, help out) way more than you talk about yourself and what you are up to (here is my blog post, watch my youtube, visit my website). Once that happens, you will see interactions come right back to you in +1s, comments, and shares."

Amanda Blain's powerful Google+ activity starts with a strong profile and beautiful cover photo (see Figure 15.4).

Figure 15.4 Amanda Blain's Google+ cover photo

Other Networks

Watch for announcements about new networks that Klout is count-ing. Also, pay attention to networks that are growing as their growth will cause them to have more bearing on your Klout Score.

CHAPTER 16

Online Collaborative Networks

If you want to go fast, go alone.
If you want to go far, go together.
—AFRICAN PROVERB

Many people increase social media engagement—and their Klout Score—by participating in online collaborative networks (OCNs). These online communities are great places to find people who have similar interests and who are willing to share your content in exchange for you sharing theirs.

Before we talk about groups that exist or how they work, let's briefly discuss the issue of whether participating in such groups is somehow "gaming the system" or unethical. The premise of this theory is that people should be 100 percent "organic" in how they get their friends and followers. For the purists, a true influencer produces great content and, entirely through his or her own interactions, motivates people to consume the content, share it, and interact with said influencer.

The truth is that even if someone's efforts are not very structured or organized, people naturally follow the principle of reciprocity to help people who help them. In other words, there exists an implied understanding that if I like your post or retweet your tweet, you are likely to do the same for me.

As defined by Wikipedia, "Reciprocity in social psychology refers to responding to a positive action with another positive action, rewarding kind actions."[1] This principle is further explained in the book *Influence: Science and Practice* by Robert B. Cialdini.[2]

We suggest that online collaborative networks are similar to leads clubs or business associations that exist in the physical world. Much like a person attends such meetings in order to exchange leads, people in OCNs "attend" in order to share social networks. A good OCN will help you build a loyal tribe of people who want to share your content such as articles, videos, audios, pictures, and events.

Following are some examples of popular OCNs. For a full listing of the most active and effective OCNs, along with discount codes for joining, visit http://KloutMatters.com/onlinenetworks.

Social Buzz Club

Created by Laura Rubinstein and Kathryn Rose, the Social Buzz Club (SBC) is a social sharing platform that makes it really easy to submit your "buzz" for sharing and to share other members' content. SBC uses points and allows you to easily submit your content such that you can customize each post. A key to getting this to count toward your Klout Score is setting up your tweets to include "via @name" or "by @name" where you use your Twitter handle in the tweet you are asking others to share.

EXPERT TIP

Key to getting this to count toward your Klout Score is setting up your tweets to include "via @name" or "by @name" where you use your name in the tweet you are asking others to share.

Another benefit of the Social Buzz Club is Social Buzz University, which provides weekly training in the various social networks, sales, marketing, and more. Currently, the training is free for those who listen to the live events—usually Thursdays at 2 p.m. (EST). Access to the recordings in the resource library is available to paid members. Since the beginning, Gina has been "Dean" of the Social Buzz University. Get the latest training at www.SocialBuzzTraining.com.

According to Social Buzz Club cofounder Laura Rubinstein, the Social Buzz Club is a platform where influencers gather and share each other's tweets, Facebook messages, and LinkedIn updates. You'll attract a wider audience and get more traffic to your site simply by using this content-sharing tool. It's a marvellous way to get others to willingly share your *great* content. This gamified platform ensures reciprocal sharing.[3]

Gina is the dean of the Social Buzz University. As of this publication date, she has no ownership in the company. However, she is a member of the Social Buzz Club.

Triberr

Triberr enables you to join various tribes by exchanging bones. By joining a tribe, you are able to plug into Triberr's system of easy social sharing. You can link your RSS feed into the tribe portal. Then, when you do a new post, tribe members can easily share it. We say "easily" with a little tongue in check. Some people—including us—find Triberr difficult to use.

Triberr recently released a plug-in for WordPress that allows you to easily share your fellow tribe members' posts when you go into your own WordPress dashboard. We expect this will lead to increased use of Triberr.

Empire Avenue

Empire Avenue (EAv) is a social collaboration network that provides you with a "stock price" based on your social influence as measured by EAv. After joining, other members can "purchase" shares in you that contribute to your "stock price." There are two primary ways that EAv helps with your Klout Score: missions and +K sharing.

One of the advantages of sharing with EAv is that you have the opportunity to network easily with people all over the world—different people than you normally interact with. One of the disadvantages of sharing with Empire Avenue is that you might not know the people who you are sharing with as well. According to Empire Avenue fan and social media guru Dwayne Kilbourne:

> *Empire Avenue is a great community where, like Klout, people can sync up their various social media profiles and receive a rating score, both for each network that is connected as well as an overall score. While different, a higher Empire Avenue virtual stock price and dividend tend to lead to a higher Klout Score. When using Empire Avenue's Missions, people can reward others via virtual currency (Eaves) in exchange for that person or brand performing some task for them, i.e., YouTube video Like, retweet, etc. Using Missions effectively can often draw more shares and overall engagement from your audience which then lends itself to both a higher Klout Score and Empire Avenue virtual stock price. Most importantly, successful implementation of Missions puts your content in front of more eyes, providing a better chance that your call to action is positively received by the other party![4]*

Facebook Groups

There are a number of Facebook groups where people participate in organized social sharing each day. In these groups, people are able to jump in to participate in "daily activities" that allow participants to share socially in a structured manner.

For example, I created a secret Facebook group years ago called the Social Media Partners. Each day we share social posts in an organized manner. It is based on reciprocity. If you are interested, send a request to www.facebook.com/groups/socialprofs.

ARE ONLINE COLLABORATION GROUPS ETHICAL?

Are online collaboration groups where people have structured reciprocation ethical? People have used IRL (in real life) structured networking groups like BNI (Business Networking International) for years. In these groups, members engage in organized lead exchanges that are somewhat similar to the social exchanges that occur in online collaborative networking groups. Much like the infamous "Google slaps" that have occurred over the years, Klout will be on the lookout for inauthentic behavior and will penalize people who appear to be attempting to game the system just for the sake of gaming the system. Klout's algorithm already accounts for "gaming" activity as it considers your score over a 90-day period and it adjusts for someone who is interacting with the same people all the time. That is to say that Klout gives more value to people who are interacting with different people.

When choosing an OCN, consider the following:

- **Size.** A group that is too big can be unwieldy and unsustainable. Find a group where you can effectively engage members for 10 to 30 minutes a day and achieve real value from your investment.
- **Time.** Spending too much time can be a real issue—we'd rather have a high bank account and a low Klout Score than the reverse.
- **Consistency.** Of course, you should never share content that is contrary to your principles. And, you should not give someone a +K or endorsement unless you have some reason to believe the person deserves it.

In summary, online collaborative networks can help you establish strong alliances with others and ultimately help you raise your Klout Score. However, they should be used carefully and judiciously.

CHAPTER 17

Myths About Boosting Your Klout Score

*I believe in everything until it's disproved. So I believe in fairies,
the myths, dragons. It all exists, even if it's in your mind.
Who's to say that dreams and nightmares
aren't as real as the here and now?[1]*
—JOHN LENNON

Any system that has a lot of followers will generate some myths that aren't quite true. Klout has attracted its own share of myths, and they need to be dealt with here. Our purpose here is not just to show what the myths are, but to correct them and to show you ways that you can build your business by doing what is right.

So let's have some fun as we examine some of the myths that are built around clout and a Klout Score.

Myth 1: Buying Twitter Followers Will Boost Your Score

This is one of the oldest tricks and schemes in the book. It flat-out doesn't work. It is based on the false idea that Klout will give you a higher score based on the number of followers you have on Twitter. This is a myth that still persists even though it has been denied in many places.

Klout does not measure your score based on the number of followers you have in Twitter. Your Klout Score is based on the amount of influence you render demonstrated by actions that others take on your behalf. This means the more people who retweet what you say, or comment about what you say, or mention you the higher your Klout Score will be.

The ugly truth about buying Twitter followers is that most of those are not real people—they are merely robots. It is very difficult to get robots to genuinely respond and interact with you!

The bottom line is you build your Klout Score by doing those activities that help you build business. That means you interact with others. It means you engage with others. It means you respond as a real, genuine human being to others.

Myth 2: Buying Friends on Facebook Will Boost Your Score

This is similar to myth number one. Klout measures real interaction with real people in genuine ways. If you try to artificially boost the number of people you have as friends, it will eventually come out in the real world that they don't exist.

Facebook is a great place to meet people and interact in the digital world. Both of us have enjoyed working with people around the world and being able to renew friendships from years ago because of Facebook. It often seems popular to deride Facebook today in the press, and we read many snarky reporters who bash Facebook at every possible chance.

Sure, Facebook has its problems, but there are a lot of advantages, and this can help you not only in your personal life but also in business. Facebook can be a great tool to help boost your Klout Score if you use it the right way. Engage with people on a real basis and keep it real. This is something that is very simple, but it is not easy. It takes discipline and work so that every day you have a presence and reach out to people helping them with valuable information. As more people get to know you on Facebook and appreciate what you are contributing, they will tell others about you, and this in turn will boost your Klout Score.

Myth 3: There Is No Way to Boost Your Klout Score

This one makes us sigh. Some people exhibit a lot of despondency and even depression when they see that their Klout Score is not going up, or in fact is going down. We can relate to that! If you work at something diligently hoping that you're doing the right thing and it still doesn't work, it becomes discouraging.

But cheer up, fellow Klout booster! By putting into place the specific steps we've recommended in this book, you should be able to see an increase in your Klout Score. It doesn't always come immediately. Sometimes it will require several weeks or months to see a difference. However, if you consistently give good, valuable content and interact with people in a pleasant, engaging way, your Klout Score is likely to improve. Can we, or anyone else, promise that if you do certain activities your Klout Score will increase? Unfortunately not. However, as we have demonstrated in this book, we have seen that doing consistently logical, reasonable business-building activities will help you to generate more business and hence generate a higher influence and Klout Score.

Myth 4: A Klout Score "Link System" Is a Great Way to Boost Your Klout Score

This silly idea has its roots in some of the "link farms" that we saw years ago with people trying to boost their SEO (search engine optimization) ratings. The idea was that many different websites would align with each other, and because Google valued links, it would drive up the search engine optimization rankings. The problem came that it was contrived and not based on sound business practices.

Today many people are entering into similar situations with Klout. They are trying to grab a group of people all of whom will promote each other and generate higher Klout Scores as a result. This might result in some temporary boost to the Klout Scores of those in the group. However, it is not sustainable.

Klout will constantly look for these "link systems" that exist and will take steps to disband them. If you are a serious thought leader and you want to build your business and credibility, this is not the approach you want to take. Yes, you do want to help others and promote those who are in similar communities as you. This is comparable to the 1960s where you might talk about a friend's sale that is going on that weekend and then a few weekends later your friend talks about your sale. This is commonsense community building where people help each other.

It might work for a while or a one-time event. However, it is always best to engage in those activities that are sustainable over the long term. Any trick or contrived system cannot last long.

Many thought leaders will help other thought leaders who have a book coming out. For example, when thought leader A has a new book coming out, many other thought leaders will agree to promote thought leader A's book to their list. This helps thought leader A, of course, but it also helps those who are followers of the other thought leaders.

Both of us enjoy hearing about new books that are coming out from people who we respect and admire. Knowing a source from whom we can find out about good new material in the form of books, audios, webinars, seminars, and other forms of education helps us. This is a genuine win-win situation.

When you regularly share valuable compelling content that you've discovered with your community, you can be seen as a valuable resource. People will see you as an excellent curator of information. You are helping two sets of people with this: (1) you are helping people who are sending out information, and (2) you are helping your community to grow. This results in a three-way win for you, for your colleagues, and for your community.

Notice that the emphasis has to be on providing good, solid content. It can't be just promotions and selling. Most reasonable business-people today understand that you do need to sell actively in order to stay in business. We've also noticed that people who do exceptionally well in business and are successful not only understand the importance of buying material, but also look forward to purchasing new learning materials so that they can become better. Something happens when you pay money for new information. Yes, free information is valuable, but when someone has to put money into the deal, it takes on a whole new dimension. It also changes the dynamics on the part of the seller. It seems that universally people realize they have to put in more value when they are selling something versus giving it away free.

Become a good curator of compelling content and valuable information for your tribe or community. Help other thought leaders and help your community by doing this—and in doing so you will help yourself.

Myth 5: You Have to Be Obsessed About Your Klout Score

The opposite is true. We admit that it can become very easy to be obsessed with developing your Klout Score. It is tempting to check it each day as it changes up or down.

A much better (and healthier!) approach is to focus on being a good social media citizen. This means being part of the discussion in those areas that are important to you. Comment on the posts of others. Retweet those tweets that resonate with you. Create compelling content that your niche will value and enjoy.

If you do these activities, and others that we've mentioned elsewhere in this book, you will find that you have the right rhythm for connecting in social media. Remember, it is a constant evaluation and testing to find out what works best for you in your unique situation.

CHAPTER 18

What Klout Doesn't Count, but We Wish It Did!

It doesn't matter which side of the fence you get off on sometimes. What matters most is getting off. You cannot make progress without making decisions.[1]
—JIM ROHN

We believe that three key areas should be measured by Klout: (1) YouTube video views, (2) podcast downloads and actual listens, and (3) blog posts read most often.

It makes no sense that YouTube channels are not ranked as a factor in building your Klout Score. Think of the Korean rapper Psy, who recently had the number one video hit on YouTube, "Gangnam Style," with over 1.6 billion views (as of this writing)! That is very influential! And yet Klout does not consider a YouTube presence as a factor in calculating a Klout Score.

In all fairness to Klout, we discussed this with Klout's chief scientist, Ding Zhou, during a visit to Klout headquarters in San Francisco. He agreed with us that YouTube is very influential and should eventually be included in a Klout Score. At this time, the YouTube API (application program interface) is complex, and the Klout scientists are working to find ways to integrate relevant signals into the Klout algorithm.[2]

Another example of a very popular YouTube presence is the video that has been wildly popular called "The Evolution of Dance." It is a video that has been very popular for many years and is performed by Judson Laipply.

Judson is a friend of ours through the National Speakers Association. He has used the popularity of his video, and other marketing strategies, to build a very successful speaking profession. He is in high demand as a thought leader. He is known as someone who makes people laugh and think.

Judson has used YouTube to get his message out and to generate a lot of business from it. The video shows a creative way to look at dance accompanied with music through the years. As we write this, it has generated over 211 million views! You would think that such a video would generate business—and a good Klout Score. Hey, Judson could probably form his own country with that large a following!

Yet, as this is being written, Judson's club score is 48. This is respectable, but it does not do justice to what his popularity has really been. We would submit that his degree of influence, generating over 211 million views, should be reflected in a much higher Klout Score.

We would argue that YouTube should be considered as part of one's overall Klout Score. We would also argue that other forms of video should be considered as well. Tools like Vimeo, Blip.tv, and many other rich sources of material should be considered when factoring Klout Score. As of this writing, YouTube and other rich educational resources are not factored into a Klout Score.

Judson is doing a lot with other areas in social media and enjoying much success. In writing this book, we had a video interview with him to talk about his "Evolution of Dance" video and what he is doing to build his own business (yes, he does talk!). This is described in more detail in the video that accompanies this book, which you can view at http://KloutMatters.com/videos-and-more or by scanning the QR code that follows with your smartphone.

We are hoping that this will be changed in the future. Yes, there will be considerations as to how to view certain videos, which ones are more relevant, and given topics, etc. We think of Stefan Molyneux, with Freedomain Radio, one of our favorite bloggers and podcasters. Stefan has the number one philosophy podcast in the world. He has generated millions of downloads of his material. To any reasonable person, this is a strong measure of influence. Yet, the work that Stefan does on YouTube does not affect his Klout Score.

If the goal of a Klout Score is to accurately measure one's digital influence, surely a case can be made for including YouTube. Joe Fernandez and the wonderful people at Klout each listened carefully as we set forth our case on these. They all agreed that YouTube views, podcast listens, and blog reads should play a factor in one's overall Klout Score. They also said they are working on that, but it will take time, largely due to some technical issues. That is encouraging.

And while we're at it, we also believe that blogs should be factored into a Klout Score. We have been fans of blogs for many years and read a wide variety of blogs on a regular basis.

Terry has had his blog since 2003 and has been able to generate much business as a result of it. The way a blog can generate business for a thought leader is that people will read the blog and get to know the author of that blog and want to do business later. For Terry this comes in the form of people buying his speaking services and his coaching services along with various products that have been produced. If you are a thought leader, you need to seriously consider producing a quality blog on a regular basis.

Having said that, it would be important for the geniuses at Klout to figure out how to make the algorithm work to factor in influential blogs. If someone has a readership of, say, 1 million readers a week, that is an important consideration for influence. Contrast that with someone who might have two or three readers over a year. The blogosphere is a wonderful place to get ideas to learn to grow and gain a competitive advantage in this hotly competitive world. We contend that consuming information from the right blogs is one of the best-kept secrets for gaining a competitive advantage, getting more business, and boosting your Klout Score.

According to Klout scientists, Tumblr is likely to be the first blog network that counts toward your Klout Score. This is because Tumblr is growing so fast and is so social-friendly. Although there is no official timeline for this, we expect it to occur before year-end 2013.[3]

The third area that is extraordinarily important in today's digital world and is not currently factored into considering one's Klout Score is podcasting. Podcasting is a way to send out messages via an audio medium in most cases. There are video podcasts that are able to send information to a lot of people in a clear way, but audio podcasting is easier to produce and easier to consume, and therefore there tend to be more audio podcasts.

Podcasting really has its roots in radio. Terry relates to this as he started in radio at WUFN–FM in Albion, Michigan, when he was 17 years old. He also worked in radio when he was in college and immediately after college worked at two radio stations in Oklahoma. Traditional radio had many elements of today's social media. There was a community around those who listen to the radio. Many people felt a part of something bigger than a radio station as they would listen avidly every day. A morning radio DJ would get attention and build the community by being witty, educational, provocative, and building an audience. Many radio stations would have occasional events where people could see the radio heroes in real life.

Think of some of the best radio programs you've listened to. If you never met the person who is the radio personality, you might not know what he or she looks like. Yet even if you don't know exactly what the person looks like, your mind will create an image of what that person "should" look like. This is part of the social world in which we live. We think visually, and we want to "see" the person that we are connecting to—even if it is just in our minds.

As radio built a community and avid followers, we see podcasts doing that today. If you listen to a podcast regularly, you begin to feel close to the speaker even though it is a one-way communication. The beauty of social media is that a true podcast today can involve listeners in the form of a variety of feedback tools.

Some of the tools that podcasters can use to connect with their community include voice mail response, Twitter handles, feedback on a website, and even good old e-mail! The more ways you can enhance the engagement and connection of the community that listens to your podcast, the better off you will be. Think of your podcast as yet another way that you can delightfully enhance the lives of those who listen to you.

We have found a tremendous amount of learning from the podcasts that we listen to on a regular basis. One of the beauties of portable technology of late is that podcasting has seen a resurgence in demand. Podcasting was big a few years ago back around 2003, 2004, and 2005. However, it dropped off moderately because it was a little too difficult to take a message as an MP3 audio file and copy it over to your device. Today, with the advancement of technology with smartphones, more people are able to listen to podcasts on their mobile phones. If you couple that with congestion on highways—which seems to increase every year!—then it makes listening to educational material imminently a greater way to learn and grow. This is another one of our little secrets on how you can achieve more influence, build your sales, and ultimately get a higher Klout Score.

We find the medium of a podcast a much better use of time than listening to the drivel on most radio stations. Think about it. If you are a thought leader, people are paying you for your thoughts. The degree to which you can create compelling content and send it out to people who are willing to purchase your ideas will determine the business success you have. The more you feed your mind with quality information, the better off you'll be.

So let's look at a scenario: if you have 30 minutes in the morning to prepare your breakfast and eat it, are you better off listening to traffic reports on the highway or hearing about a terrible crime that happened over on the south side of town last night? Think of this versus spending time with a great thought leader who can teach you valuable content. A big part of success and adventure in life is knowing where you have to say no. You have to say no to many B and B+ activities so that you can focus on the A and A+ activities. Be honest now, is knowing about the latest crime on the south side of town more important than you growing and stretching your mind by learning valuable new skills to help your customers?

We're not saying that you should become an ostrich and remain unaware of what's happening in the world—or your local community. We are saying that you need to focus your attention predominately on those key areas that will help you be of better benefit to your paying customers. We have found we can gain sufficient knowledge of what's happening in the world and what we need to know by doing a quick read of news from a few reliable, reputable news sources online. Be aware of what's happening in our world. Just be sure to focus your attention on those areas that are most relevant to your buyers.

Time is your most precious resource. Yes, it is important to know what's going on in your local community and in the world. However, is it the best use of your time to listen to the current weather over and over along with the current political hot topic of the moment? Unless you speak directly about those topics, wouldn't it be better for you to invest your time, money, and effort into listening to some of the great minds that have ever lived and that are living today about areas that can help your community?

What does all this have to do with your Klout Score?

Plenty!

Make it a daily practice to bathe your mind with good quality audio. Instead of listening to the clutter, confusion, and depressing news coming out of most radio stations, spend that time bathing your mind in some of the greatest thoughts and ideas of all time. Make it a point to listen not only to current ideas related to your subject topic but also to the classics. Much wisdom is contained in works of art from those who left us long ago. By saturating your mind with good principles and knowledge gleaned from the classics, you will gain a strong competitive advantage in this world. Think of the benefits of being able to relate a story of how Napoleon used certain principles to win battles. The wise thought leader will then take those principles that Napoleon used and apply them to real-world problems today. As you do this on a regular basis, you will increase your influence and, yes, increase your Klout Score.

Be sure to check out Appendix A of this work for some of the podcasts that we listen to and recommend. We'd also like to hear from you. What are some of your favorite must-listen-to podcasts? You can leave your comments on our Klout Matters website. As we've mentioned before in this book, visit the website we have created to keep you up to date with Klout changes and how to raise your Klout Score by being a good social media citizen. Visit http://KloutMatters.com.

We hope that Klout will eventually include podcasts as part of the overall scoring system. For thought leaders in particular, podcasts are an area of influence that need to be factored into the overall equation.

For now, we'd recommend that if you use YouTube, podcasting, and/or blogging to keep it up even if it doesn't affect your Klout Score right now. While you use those channels, be sure to encourage your viewers, listeners, and readers to send you info through those Klout-observing channels like Twitter, Facebook, LinkedIn, and others. Ask your viewers, listeners, and readers to comment on your Facebook page or to send you a tweet. This way you can get some Klout juice from your efforts.

But whether or not Klout considers it as part of the overall Klout Score equation, take this as an opportunity for you, as a thought leader, to gain a competitive advantage and become a better person. As you saturate your mind with good content from some of the best blogs, some of the best podcasts, and some of the best YouTube channels out there, you will increase your knowledge and comprehension of valuable, compelling content. Think of it like going to the "University of You."

The University of You is a university that we all need to attend to be competitive today. You are the professors (yes, all of them). You are the one who determines the curriculum. You are also the student. Attending the University of You requires an enormous amount of discipline. You have to make sure you go to "class" on a daily basis. Even though it might be easier to do something else, you need to make sure you read those important blog posts, listen to those important podcasts, and watch those important videos.

Also, remember that you never "graduate" from the University of You. There's always new classes that you need to attend. Yes, your ongoing education is imperative for success today and in the future.

In a world where knowledge matters enormously, you will have a competitive advantage sitting at the feet of some of the most brilliant thought leaders in the world. And a great thing about attending the University of You is that you get to select just the material that you want to learn.

CHAPTER 19

With Whom Should You Engage?

My belief has long been that if you just get out there and keep doing good and stay active within your areas of speciality and passion, all the numbers will take care of themselves.[1]
—MARI SMITH

Focus on interaction and engagement—not broadcasting.

This is what Klout is all about. Klout is not about gaming the system and doing certain tricks in order to boost your score. Boosting your Klout Score is about engaging in those activities that involve interaction and that are important for marketing in any environment.

Another controversial area of working with Klout is "Whom should you engage with?" In other words, should you interact with everyone, or should you interact only with people who have high Klout Scores?

Your Klout Score will increase if you interact with people who have higher Klout Scores than you. At first brush, this almost seems like a distasteful digital way of preferring the "rich" over the "poor."

But let's step back and think about the concept of who you should engage with for interaction because it is very important.

It is natural that if you hang around people who are more influential, you will become more influential. But since everyone knows the way the game is played, aren't those with higher influence going to want to stay away from people with lower Klout Scores? Are we creating a stratified system of interaction in the social media world? Whatever happened to the democratization of ideas?

You can see how this argument could get very ugly after a while. However, there is a solution and a decent, civilized way to deal with it.

We have found that by providing information, we are able to garner the respect of many other people. You want to get the attention of many people who are in your target market. This includes people with both higher and lower scores than yours. But the market has a way of self-correcting. Those with higher Klout Scores are going to be aware that others who have lower scores are trying to interact with them. Many times, people with lower Klout Scores possibly want to "use" those who have higher Klout Scores.

We have seen the equivalent of this in the real world from our speaking experience. Often, after a celebrity speaks, he or she is swamped by people. There's nothing wrong with this, as people want to shake the hand of someone that they admire or a speaker that they greatly appreciated. This is actually a good thing for many speakers as they receive positive feedback this way.

However, it can get very ugly when we see certain individuals who try to monopolize the time of the celebrity and only want to talk about themselves. I've seen many cases when there will be a long line of people talking to a given celebrity of the moment after that celebrity's speech. Such obnoxious persons want to monopolize the celebrity's time and not have any concern for anyone else there who also wants to talk with the celebrity. These people often think that they are the only ones who matter in life. They have narcissism on steroids.

However, celebrities are usually not stupid and can often act to correct the situation. They can see a fake coming a mile away. In the real world, those smart celebrities who have experienced this often are able to politely nudge the offending person aside and be able to help other people as well. The offending narcissists are quickly detected for who they really are.

That is what happens in the real world, and we see an equivalent reaction happening online now. There are many who understand that interacting with high Klout Score people can help to boost their own score. The astute high influential person will recognize such people for who they are and what they're doing. A high Klout Score person can then choose either not to interact with the obnoxious offender or to interact in a very constrained and limited way.

So what is the answer if your Klout Score is low and you really do want to interact with someone who has a higher Klout Score? The answer is not a mystery. It goes back to what we all have known all along and are talking about in this book. You must provide genuine value and compelling content for interaction and engagement.

The best way to get through to a famous person, using social media and in the real world, is to understand the person's needs and how you can help him or her. Hey, we're all human beings! We all have needs, wants, and desires, and we all look forward to being around people who can help us. This means you have to do your homework.

If there is a celebrity you want to interact with on social media, get to know the interests of that celebrity. Join groups and contribute where that celebrity visits and is active online. Your Klout Score will increase as you interact with people who have higher Klout Scores. The key is to provide value to them as they interact on social media.

Another good way to build your influence and ultimately to enhance your Klout Score is to interact with others who are respected by that celebrity. For instance, suppose you want to get to know Mary, who is a local celebrity. Find someone who Mary admires and respects, and then ask that person to introduce you to Mary. Being introduced by someone people respect holds a lot more credibility for you than you walking up out of the blue and introducing yourself.

Another way to do this would be to be seen in those places where that celebrity hangs out. A digital equivalent of this would be to find out what podcasts that celebrity listens to and make plans to participate in those podcasts. If there is a given blog that you know that celebrity regularly reads, then do what you can to become a guest blogger on that site.

You're probably getting the idea by now that it is not some trick or technique that allows you to get through to people. It comes from genuinely helping them and providing serious value over an extended period. Building genuine respect and credibility in the minds of others requires consistent, positive action over time. It is not a one-time event. Narcissistic people who run up to a celebrity and try to monopolize his or her time at a public event are quickly seen for who they really are. Don't be that person.

Instead, do your homework. Study the high Klout Score person you want to meet and get to know the person's areas of interest, desires, and needs. Become the solution for his or her current problems. Build your credibility so that it is known that you are competent in this area and can render serious help.

This takes consistent practice over time. We meet many people as we travel and speak around the world at various conventions. Many times we meet someone at a convention and that person tries to impress us by telling us who he or she is. That is nice as far as it goes. But those who stand out in our minds most favorably are those whom we see many times in several different venues over an extended period. That builds credibility, and it shows that the person is going to be serious and around for the long run. There are many people we see one time, and they are very excited about getting to know us—however, we don't see them again very often. In order to make a strong favorable impression with someone, it takes time and effort done consistently.

Never underestimate the value of constant and regular preparation. Terry often shares a story about how he was able to be on a panel with a person whom he admired and for whom he voted for the office of president of the United States.

Not many people get a chance to meet and spend quality time with the person they have voted for in a presidential election. Terry was able to do this when he was asked to be on a panel with Harry Browne, the Libertarian party candidate for president in 1996 and 2000. Terry was to be on the panel for this conference because he had met the person in charge of it, Mark Skousen, and Mark had asked Terry to be on the panel. The event was called FreedomFest, and was held in Las Vegas, Nevada, in 2003.

During the public interaction with the other three members of the panel, Terry was able to joke with Harry Browne and talk about what Harry had done as a candidate for president. When the session was concluded, Harry asked Terry if he had some time to talk about topics of mutual interest.

At that point, Harry and Terry went to an out-of-the-way location and talked for an hour and a half about the business of professional speaking. It seems that Harry was very interested in working more in the profession of speaking and wanted to work with more speakers bureaus. This is something that Terry had been doing for many, many years, so he provided Harry Browne with some helpful tips.

The result was that Harry Browne was able to get some additional business from Terry's ideas and the two forged a friendship that lasted until Harry's death a few years later.

The interaction and time spent with Harry Browne was not something that was planned or contrived. It was not something that Terry initiated. It was generated because Harry Browne, a celebrity in that event, saw that Terry could provide value and asked Terry to join him for a discussion. This often happens in the world of social media. Be in the right groups. Notice what is of interest to people with whom you want to interact. Give positive interaction to their tweets by retweeting, "like" their posts and pictures on Facebook, and do what you can to help them. It has to be done in a genuine, authentic way to work in the real world and in social media. Done properly and authentically, this can help you and your Klout Score in the long run.

Think through the developments that took place to make this happen and use it as a learning point to build your own network with highly influential people. Terry had done his homework before the event. He knew a lot about the speaking business as well as the topics of liberty and freedom around which that conference was centered. These areas were of great interest to Harry Browne. Terry also made the connection with Mark Skousen, who graciously asked him to be on the panel. Terry was able to position himself as an authority, even as an equal on the panel, with Harry Browne. By the way, the two other people on the panel were Sharon Harris, the head of a prominent libertarian organization, and Marshall Fritz, a well-known figure in the libertarian movement at the time.

You want to position yourself as an authority and an expert in a given field. Celebrities like to be around other celebrities. The nice thing about the world today is that you can be a celebrity in a small field by learning some particular areas of expertise.

Yes, this is being a "big fish in a small pond," and it works very well today. Become an expert in key areas that people in your community want to know about. Do your homework. Study. Listen to podcasts. Read the best blogs. Watch the best videos on YouTube. All of this is part of your educational process.

A strong case can be made for becoming the big fish in a small pond first. Those who are the gatekeepers and have the ability to promote you to be a big fish in a big pond like to see success in the "small pond" area first. As an example, suppose your target market is accountants. If you desire to be positioned with the American Institute of Certified Public Accountants (AICPA), then a good place to start is at the local level. If there is a meeting in your city, get to know people there and find out when they would have a need for a speaker at their local event. Many organizations are desperately looking for speakers for their weekly or monthly meetings, and this is a great place to demonstrate your competence.

Once you have been there and demonstrated competence, you gain a following. You can then move from the local level to the state level and perhaps later on the national level. Yes, you have to pay your dues. Much like many newly minted MBAs who want to start as CEO on their first job, many people want to start at the top as an internationally known thought leader. It seldom, if ever, works this way.

Start by providing value to people at the local level. Work diligently and leverage what you're doing to be on a national scope. Today this is easier than ever before. In the past, you would need to speak at the local level, then try, somehow, to get into the state level, then try, somehow, to get into the national level. This process could take many years to develop.

Today, you can leapfrog over the traditional means. Consider speaking at the local level and make sure that you have it recorded on video. That video can then be placed on your YouTube channel. If you have a series of videos on different topics that are of interest to your target market, you can be sure that those at the national level will watch for you. This is a great way to generate new business.

Since Klout does not (as we write this) use a YouTube channel to factor into your overall Klout Score, you'll want to further enhance it elsewhere. A great way to do that is to make sure you send out notices on Twitter, on Facebook, and on LinkedIn that point to your presentation that is available on YouTube.

Those who are meeting planners and are looking for new presenters will do searches to find out who is providing valuable content. As they see that you are providing valuable content, they will want to follow your work. Of course, this will enhance your Klout Score. More important, it will help build your business.

Once you have that expertise in a major area that buyers want, make sure you position yourself in front of key people whom you want to meet. Do your homework again. You not only have to have the expertise, you have to be able to use that expertise to help those celebrities solve their problems.

It might seem somewhat daunting at first, but really this is a marvelous feature of today's world. Because of the wealth of information available on the Internet, you can research and become an expert in many different topics. You have to be willing to put in the time for study to make it happen. Any good thought leader today worth his or her salt will budget hours of study time each day. There is no getting around it. You must remain current and valuable to the marketplace with your ideas.

The positive part of this is that, as a thought leader, you probably enjoy studying and learning already. Develop the necessary discipline to focus your mind on a given topic every day.

The very good news is that you should be thankful you're alive today versus trying to do this many years ago. You will enhance your success by following the steps we have just laid out. Start by presenting, having it recorded, putting it on YouTube, and then referencing it through channels like Twitter, Facebook, LinkedIn, and other social media tools. This type of promotion was impossible many years ago and very difficult just a few short years ago. Today you cannot only do it much easier and cheaper, but also it is more commonly used by buyers to find their vendors. As a thought leader, you're better off today than ever before!

It is most important that you be seen as an expert and an authority in your field of choice. The late great Earl Nightingale, called the "Dean of Personal Development," had some very interesting thoughts on this topic. Earl Nightingale would say in his recordings that you can become an expert in any field if you devote a minimum of one hour a day, five days a week for five years to learning that topic.

We don't know about the exact number of hours needed because we're sure that it varies from profession to profession. However, Earl Nightingale had it right in devoting consistent, regular study time to becoming an expert in a given field. This is what separates the winners from losers.

Losers expect instant results and instant gratification. Losers are not willing to pay the price for success. They will get enthused at the meeting and claim that they will do something. However, the real work gets done on those mornings when you wake up, it's cold outside, you don't feel very good, and you'd rather sleep than study. Losers and successful people both have days like this.

The difference comes in that successful people are willing to force themselves to do the things that they might not want to do at that moment. They have a vision for a greater goal, and that vision helps them do the difficult task of the moment. If you consistently study valuable material that is worthwhile to others and commit yourself to learning, you will succeed. This is a simple formula, and yet it is not easy.

As you commit yourself to learning valuable material that is useful to others, you will become more knowledgeable of what works and is successful in your field of endeavor. The beautiful part of this is that it becomes a cumulative process. The toughest part will be at the beginning. You will need to learn how to discipline yourself. You will need to learn what to do. Most important, you will need to learn what *not* to do.

Take these rules that apply to real-life connections and apply them to the digital world as well. Think about the celebrities who you want to connect with on a regular basis. Find out what their needs are and how you can help them. Take particular interest in celebrities who are launching a new book or a new webinar or have a project that they're involved with where you can help.

When you see an area where you can help a celebrity, give the person real value. Part of this value would be sending out a notice to a large group of people that you have accumulated as part of your community or tribe. Think about how you might be able to interview the celebrity to give him or her added value.

The digital world is not that much different from real-life activities today. People always need help in certain key areas. Find those areas where you can help and render assistance, and then do it.

As you do this, you become seen as a resource to highly influential people. That is what you want in life. You want to be seen as the resource to go to when people need to get things accomplished.

This is all part of the process, and being willing to pay the price in this process is the ticket for success. As you become successful in this area, you will increase in influence and your business will grow, and you will ultimately get a higher Klout Score.

Will there be a price that you have to pay?

Absolutely!

Is it worth it?

You bet!

CHAPTER 20

So What Is a Thought Leader to Do?

I'm not sure how important the Klout Score actually is,
but if enough people say it's important others will begin to believe
it's important. Which came first, the chicken or the egg?[1]
—JOEL COMM

Today Klout is the largest and most respected measuring tool for considering one's influence. Love it or hate it, this tool is one that every marketer and thought leader needs to be aware of and embrace. Yes, Klout has its detractors and those who think that it is "evil." Yeah, even if something is "evil," if it is the dominant force in the industry, it is a force that all marketers and thought leaders need to be aware of.

Influence is a difficult topic to measure. It is squishy with all kinds of nonquantifiable variables attached to it. Questions like, "Is this person like me?" will always affect a decision. "Do I like the way this person comes across in a subjective way?" is always going to be a consideration when making decisions.

The key importance of influence is ultimately persuasion. If someone has influence over a given area, does he or she have the ability to persuade others to take positive action? Determining who is most influential, and therefore most persuasive, is the key goal of influence marketing.

It is always fascinating to be able to point out a celebrity saying, "Hey, there's so-and-so, the popular movie actor, political star, hit musician, etc." We could measure that those celebrities do have a high influence factor. This can be done by the number of people who "like" this person on Facebook or who follow a given person on Twitter.

However, in business, what ultimately matters is the ability of a key person to persuade and influence business decisions. This primarily means sales.

Klout measures the amount of influence someone has by that person's ability to persuade others to take action. This is good and a step in the right direction. In business, we need more than people clicking on the screen or advocating that they "like" someone.

Ultimately, in business, you need sales in order to sustain your presence. Without sales, it really doesn't matter how many "likes" you have or how many people are following you. The cold, hard reality is that it doesn't matter what your Klout Score is if your bank account is empty! This is most important for all thought leaders, and any business enterprise, to bear in mind.

At the same time, we cannot dismiss Klout as irrelevant. In today's marketplace, it is a huge factor that buyers will use to determine whom they will spend money with for a given project or event.

Don't become like the cynics who criticize Klout incessantly. One has to wonder what might be going on inside their own minds about this. Are they doing the digital equivalent of "taking their ball and bat and going home" simply because they don't like their score? Whenever you read a post or hear a podcast that is deriding not only Klout, but any other tool out there, be sure to go deeper and examine the root causes of why the writer is expressing these opinions. Taking the posts you read with a grain of salt is usually a healthy intellectual exercise. This is a good practice to develop critical thinking, no matter how you've been exposed to new material.

The essence of measuring influence is also very difficult because of the kind of influence that is exerted in the real world. Someone might be influential as a celebrity known to millions of people, but we have to ask if that influence and degree of recognition is enough to persuade people to take a specific buying action.

For instance, if you see a basketball star who is recommending a pair of shoes, are you likely to buy? The evidence tends to suggest yes. However, if that same basketball star recommends a specific local car dealership, mutual fund, or a law firm, is that person going to be equally influential? One would question if we would take advice about choosing a mutual fund from someone merely because that person can shoot baskets very well.

This shows that there are two types of influence. One type of influence is general, and the other is specific. Going back to our hypothetical basketball star, this person might be influential regarding some sneakers, given that jumping and wearing sneakers is a part of being a basketball player. However, when it comes down to selecting which dealership in my local town I might use to buy my new car, that basketball star might have zero relevance to my decision.

A much more trusted influencer to me might be someone like a trusted friend who has had experiences similar to mine. If you have a friend or a friend of a friend who recently purchased a car in your town, that person would usually have more influence than a well-known basketball player.

Yes, influence is indeed a very slippery science. There is a lot of "squishiness" associated with it. What Klout and other measuring tools set out to do today is to quantify the process. Yes, quantification does have a lot of merit. Thought leaders today need to pay attention to this new form of measurement. But mere quantification is not the only consideration we need to make. Someone can have a high quantitative score and yet still be very low on persuasion.

Ultimately, persuasive ability is a key to success both in life and in business. One can have a very low Klout Score and still remain persuasive. One might not be particularly influential in a general sense, like a well-known basketball star. However, if the same person is persuasive on a personal level, that makes a big difference.

A business today would be wise to search not only for those who have a large following, but for those who can actually influence purchases. Those who can persuade others to make a purchase of a product or service have what really matters—Klout—and a higher Klout Score!

For those of us in the personal service areas, it is most important to be influential on a situational basis. That means that each context is different. You might have been a great speaker for the audience last week in a given town, but what matters to the new audience this week, in a different town, is how you do there.

By practicing the skills and knowledge-enhancing methods we've described in this book, you will be able to continually add to your knowledge base of relevant data for adding new customers. You will not go wrong if you're continually seeking out solutions for your clients. Add relevant knowledge to your personal information and know what you can do to translate that information into solutions for your customers. Your Klout Score can go up because of that. You need to know about your Klout Score and be cognizant of where it is on a regular basis.

From the buyer's point of view, influence will take on a much more quantitative point of view in the future. Buyers are under increased pressure to make the right decision when hiring vendors. For instance, when meeting planners are selecting the speaker to use for their next convention, they want to make sure that they have proof as to why this person is better than another. Meeting planners would feel better about their decision using a reliable source like Klout to help quantify their ultimate selection.

Brands want to know who is more influential concerning their particular product. This means that they are going to increasingly look toward those who have a larger following, more influence, and thus a higher Klout Score. Is it an exact science? Absolutely not! However, any thought leader today must be aware of the importance of the quantitative analysis that is going on in anticipating whom buyers will select.

We have enjoyed having you with us on this journey. The process of increasing your influence is always ongoing. What works today might not necessarily work tomorrow. We all know that technology becomes obsolete very quickly and there is always a new "shiny object" to be had.

On this journey, we have shown you not only some of the current new "shiny objects" but more important the principles that will work now and into the future. Focus more on the principles that last than on a new "geegaw" of the moment. You will not go wrong basing your business on sound, time-honored principles.

We wish you much continued success on your journey. We also hope that we get a chance to engage with you either online or in the real world!

Engage!
—CAPTAIN JEAN-LUC PICARD, USS ENTERPRISE, *STAR TREK: THE NEXT GENERATION, SAID BY ACTOR PATRICK STEWART AT THE CLOSE OF MOST EPISODES*

Podcasts We Recommend

Podcasts come and go, so some of these might have "gone off the radar" since we published. Also, there are many other podcasts that are very good. Please share with us your favorite podcasts on our website, http://KloutMatters.com.

When you're looking for quality educational material in audio format, podcasts can't be beat. The ease of consuming podcasts while you're engaging in other activities can be extraordinarily beneficial. Why just listen to the same old songs on the radio over and over rather than have your mind saturated with good quality information? We have personally listened to each of the podcasts listed here, and we recommend them. We look forward to hearing from you with additional ideas on our Facebook group (www.Facebook.com/groups/raiseyourkloutscore) and website (http://KloutMatters.com).

Podcast	Where to Find	Comments
The Thomas Jefferson Hour	iTunes, www. jeffersonhour.org	This is from Clay Jenkinson, an award-winning humanities scholar who portrays Jefferson and comments, as Jefferson, on contemporary topics. Excellent ideas on history, living and hot topics.
Internet Business Mastery	iTunes, www. InternetBusiness Mastery.com	Great ideas for breaking from the 9-5 job and starting your own online business. Hosted by "Jeremy and Jason"
Marketing Over Coffee	iTunes, Marketing OverCoffee.com	Hot topics and ideas on marketing and doing Social Media for Business. Hosted by John Wall and Christopher Penn.
Smart Passive Income	http://www.smart passiveincome. com/	Pat Flynn helps with interviews and real-world advice on building your business.
SocialMedia Marketing	iTunes, www. socialmedia examiner.com	Michael Stelzner focuses on doing business with Social Media on this site. Great interviews and great content.

Podcast	Where to Find	Comments
HBR Ideacast	iTunes http://blogs.hbr.org/ideacast/	Audio supplement from Harvard Business Review with additional insights that complement what is covered in the current month's publication.
This is Your Life, with Michael Hyatt	iTunes, http://michaelhyatt.com/thisisyourlife	Great ideas on marketing as well as practical living.
Get it Done Guy's Quick and Dirty Tips	iTunes, http://getitdone.quickanddirtytips.com/bio	Stever Robbins shares practical advice on how to be more efficient in a fun, witty manner.
Terry Brock's podcast	www.TerryBrock.com, iTunes	Hey, this is one we have to recommend to you! Great ideas and you'll love it!
Common Sense with Dan Carlin	http://www.dancarlin.com/disp.php/cs, iTunes	Not-so-common insights into philosophy, history and current events. Makes us think.
Wall Street Journal This Morning	iTunes www.WSJ.com	This is the recording from the current morning's show. Nice in that it is fast-paced, concise and always has relevant stories.
Six Pixels of Separation	http://www.twistimage.com/blog/ iTunes	Mitch Joel does some great interviews and shares his insights about marketing.
Mixergy	iTunes, http://mixergy.com/homepage/?awt_m=8VLnYI2SOy&awt_email=ssasdf%40dkd%2ecom	Andrew Warner shares insights from interviewing various successful entrepreneurs.
Duct Tape Marketing	iTunes, http://www.ducttapemarketing.com/	John Jantsch shares ideas on marketing and building your business.
Keen Talks	http://keentalks.com/all/	Lectures and videos on a variety of topics. Good source of richness for your intellectual diet!

YouTube and Other Videos
We Recommend

YouTube is an excellent place for learning new material. Many thought leaders consider it the "University of What We Need to Know" today. We have found it to be a tremendous source of learning and growth as we watch interviews and listen to commentaries that we would not be able to get otherwise.

We encourage you, as fellow thought leaders, to make YouTube a regular part of your intellectual diet to watch quality educational videos. When you can experience the emotion and the sights and sounds that come from videos, you can learn a lot. Use this as a way to review some of the best speakers and authors who are alive today, and even some who were able to be recorded before they left us. Make it a point to include YouTube as a regular part of your intellectual diet. You will be a better thought leader because of this, and you will thank us. You're welcome.

We'd love to hear from you on other videos and regular channels that you have found to be helpful as a thought leader. Please leave your comments on our Facebook page and on the website for this book.

As you work with videos on YouTube and other channels, you will find that often there is a single very good video. It might not be part of a series or even belong to a channel. That is why the search engine feature of YouTube is particularly helpful. Think of a topic that you want to know more about and then put that topic into the search engines feature of YouTube.

We have found this enormously helpful when we were preparing for speeches and needed to write blogs. By keying in some given topics and several relevant keywords, YouTube's search feature helped us to locate information that would not have been available otherwise.

Some of the most useful information can come from conferences and panels. This might have been a one-time event where four experts got together for a given panel at a given convention. By watching the video on YouTube, you're able to tap into information that might not be available to others so easily. We are all familiar with Google search, but not as many use YouTube for searching to gather information. This could give you a competitive advantage when your competition does not search YouTube and has not been able to see the kind of information available.

Think of it as a way that you can easily and quickly find out what some of the best minds have said in important conventions around the world. By using the right strategy, you can be involved in key conferences and listen to key thought leaders around the world at no cost to you. Rather than spending thousands of dollars on transportation, lodging, and all the costs associated with being at an event, you can access the information that is vital by knowing the right way to search.

Of course, having this information and being able to disseminate it helps you to increase your influence. As you increase your influence, you will be able to attract more followers, more business, and ultimately raise your Klout Score.

We look forward to hearing from you and getting your comments on videos that you found to be particularly helpful. This is where our Facebook page and website will become particularly useful to you as a resource. As you contribute to the knowledge base and read what others have said and comment on that, you'll be able to gain a lot of information and increase your status in the community. And yes, you can probably increase your Klout Score by participating in our Facebook page!

Here is a list of some of the most popular YouTube channels and video sites that we visit. We really look forward to hearing from you and getting your comments.

Video Channel	Where To Find It	Comments
Terry's YouTube Channel	YouTube.com/ TerryLBrock	Of course, we're biased but this is packed with over 400 great videos. Check it out.
Inc. Magazine	http://www.you tube.com/user/ incmagazine	Great ideas for small businesses— and entrepreneurial thinkers
Entrepreneur Magazine	http://www.you tube.com/user/ Entrepreneur Online	Good source of ideas and relevant information for small business leaders.
Prosperity TV	http://www.you tube.com/user/ randygage	Randy Gage shares his ideas on achieving success. Good source of ideas for thought leaders
Freedomain Radio	http://www.you tube.com/user/ stefbot	Largest philosophy site in the world. Great ideas on building your own podcast and web video presence.
Harvard Business Review	http://www.you tube.com/user/ harvardbusiness	Strong videos on a variety of topics to give thought leaders the spark of an idea or reference.

Video Channel	Where To Find It	Comments
Wharton Business School	http://www.you tube.com/user/ thewhartonschool	Get some great education at Wharton on business and more.
Stanford Business School	http://www.you tube.com/user/ stanfordbusiness	Stanford Business School ideas on growing business
TED Talks Videos	http://www.you tube.com/user/ TEDtalksDirector	Some of the best minds in the world share ideas on a variety of subjects
Big Think	http://www.you tube.com/user/ bigthink	Ideas from thought leaders from around the world on a variety of topics

Blogs We Recommend

If you're looking for the secret treasure trove for gaining a competitive advantage in business and connecting more with people, here is your solution. Reading quality educational blogs is a key for expanding your mind to see new possibilities. Those who succeed today are those who continue to stretch their mind and learn new material from a variety of different perspectives.

Yes, you need to create your own blog. Build on top of the blogs that are doing well and are making an impact. Even with all the audio, video, and other sources for media today, blogging remains the king. More information is sent via blogs.

As a thought leader, you need to read many blogs as well as create your own. You'll learn a lot about what works and what is considered "best practices" by reading those we list at the end of this appendix and others. Apply the principles to your own blog, and you'll begin to see results.

We have found that by reading a variety of different blogs with different opinions, we're able to see what is happening in the world from a much broader perspective. In today's world blogs are an integral part of how information is disseminated. To be an effective thought leader you need to stretch your mind and grow by reading a lot of material from a variety of sources.

Some people will make the mistake of reading only in their industry. This creates a perspective that is very insular. Often we see industries where many people are reading the same material over and over and just quoting the mantras that are believed to be true in that industry. Innovators are those who reach out to other industries to find applications that can be modified to fit into their own.

We could write a whole book on the importance of reading and experiencing life from many different perspectives. Suffice it to say that if you are a thought leader or a small business person or engaged in business in any way today, you benefit most when you continually learn from a variety of sources.

In this appendix we list several blogs that we find enjoyable. This list is infinitely expandable and constantly changing. Yes, some of the blogs we list here might have gone out of business and are no longer being published by the time you read this. Also there will be blogs that have emerged since we wrote this that are worthy of your consideration.

View this list as a good starting point. Of course, you can't read every blog that is out there every day. We have heard that there are no less than 3 to 4 million blogs available in the blogosphere. Frankly, we don't think anyone knows the exact number, and even if there was an exact number it would be changing constantly.

Think of it like walking into the largest library in the world and wanting to read every book. Even the fastest speed reader or photo reader would not be able to keep up with it all. That can seem a little inundating at times. Don't let the mass of information overwhelm you.

A good approach we have found that is embraced by many thought leaders is to find those few select blogs that you consider your "must-read" blogs for your intellectual diet. Realize that this list is constantly changing and being modified based on variables like the relevance of that blog to what you're working on at the moment, the current benefits that you get from that blog, and if the blog itself stays in business.

Some blogs make a point to have new content available on a regular basis. Our friend Alan Stevens, a UK-based consultant and professional speaker, puts out his blog called The Media Coach every week on Friday. Alan is a trained professional journalist, and he takes pride in keeping that deadline on a regular basis.

Another one of our friends, Mike Rayburn from Las Vegas, publishes what he calls his "wheneverly" newsletter. Mike publishes this whenever he feels like it.

As a thought leader who wants to grow in influence, you need to read from a variety of these blogs. As you tap into new ideas, you will attract new markets, hence building your followers and building your Klout Score. Regularly reading blogs is a fundamental element of your intellectual diet as a thought leader.

We look forward to hearing from you about these blogs and others on our website and our Facebook page. Keep experimenting and have fun! You will find much enjoyment and learning as you enrich your life through reading a variety of blogs that can help you become more of the person you want to be.

Blog	Where to Find It	Comments
Terry Brock's Blog	www.TerryBrock.com	Lots of ideas on marketing, technology, and personal development, and yes, we're rather biased toward this one!
Gina Carr's Blog	www.GinaCarr.com	Lots of updated ideas you can use to build your business. And yes, we are biased toward this one as well!
Social Media Examiner	http://www.socialmediaexaminer.com	This is a must-read for anyone interested in social media and growing your Klout Score. Packed with great ideas from a variety of authors covering many topics related to social media.
Mark W. Schaefer's Blog	http://www.businessesgrow.com	Refreshing "out of the box" ideas on how to grow your business. Mark also talks about influence and Klout here. Always a worthwhile read.

Blog	Where to Find It	Comments
The Sales Lion	http://www.thesaleslion.com	Marcus Sheridan comes from a real-world perspective. Not just theory, he shows how he transformed his business and how you can as well.
Jeff Bullas's Site	http://www.jeffbullas.com	Always packed with great ideas, this PR genius shares ideas related to social media.
Amy Porterfield's Site	http://www.amyporterfield.com/2012/08/3-ways-to-super-charge-fan-engagement-on-facebook	Amy Porterfield is a prominent expert on Facebook and how to build your fan base. She shows many ways to add value for your visitors and to subsequently build your Klout Score.
Mari Smith	http://www.marismith.com	Mari is well known in the social media community, and her own Klout Score testifies to that. Not only is her site packed with great ideas for social media, but she is one of the kindest people you'll ever meet.
Chris Brogan	http://www.chrisbrogan.com	Chris Brogan is one of the best! He knows social media, business, and how to help you become more successful. He stresses reality and how to build your community.
Mitch Joel, Six Pixels of Separation	http://www.twistimage.com/blog	We love his thought process. Known as a guru in social media, you can learn a lot from Mitch Joel.
Laissez Faire Book Club	http://lfb.org/blog	Innovative marketing ideas and lots of references for economic, philosophical, and real-world living thought.
Gigaom	http://gigaom.com	Tech source for new information. If you are a thought leader in the community of tech, this is a regular must-read!

Blog	Where to Find It	Comments
Mashable	http://mashable.com	Pete Cashmore built this from scratch and provides regular news material worth knowing about technology, social media, and more.
Techcrunch	http://techcrunch.com	Stay updated on technology. This is a great tool to make it happen.
Mark Sanborn's Blog	http://www.mark-sanborn.com/blog	If you work in the leadership or customer service space, this is a source you want to know. Powerful ideas from Mark Sanborn.
Bob Burg's Blog	http://www.burg.com/blog	A thought leader in personal development, Bob Burg continues to have great ideas on how to connect with people. Follow his principles and your influence will increase.
Randy Gage's Prosperity Blog	http://www.burg.com/blog	Watch the videos and read the blog about prosperity and thinking. As a thought leader, watch what Randy Gage is doing and think about the principles. Both can help you as a thought leader.
Success Blog from Lisa Jimenez	http://www.rx-success.com/blog	Lisa Jimenez talks about the principles of success and how to think of it.
ProBlogger	http://www.problogger.net	Darren Rouse has created what many considered the ultimate blog on blogging. Learn how-tos and more here.
CopyBlogger	http://www.copyblogger.com/blog	Brian Clark has put together a blog rich with details on how to build your reputation and influence in blogging.
B2B Marketing	http://www.b2bmarketinginsider.com	Michael Brenner has put together one of the foremost blogs in business-to-business marketing. Great ideas for that space and others!

Blog	Where to Find It	Comments
AT&T's Networking Exchange Blog	http:// networking exchangeblog. att.com	Keep up with mobility, security, and cloud computing on this blog where Terry was editor-in-chief once. Great ideas from a variety of experts.
Marc and Angel Hack Life	http://www. marcandangel.com	This is a delightful site packed with lots of practical how-tos for living your life your way. Thought leaders will love the workable ideas put forth.
Content Marketing Blog	http://content marketing institute.com/ author/joepulizzi	Joe Pulizzi is known as a content marketing expert. Thought leaders create content and use it to build influence and Klout Score. This is a great reference to learn what works and what doesn't.
Seth Godin's Blog	http://sethgodin. typepad.com	Seth Godin is known as one of the gurus in marketing and blogging. His blog is a must-read for thought leaders.
Jay Baer's Blog	http://www. convinceand convert.com	Brilliant marketing insights about helping, not selling in social media. Good social media principles in abundance.

Resources for Building Your Business

You know that building your Klout Score is really all about engaging with more people in a meaningful way. Sometimes having the extra tools can give you a competitive advantage and make it a lot easier for you.

Here are some resources we have encountered that have helped us and others. Of course, resources like this continue to change and evolve all the time. We know that as soon as we publish this some can be out of date and no longer exist. In addition, important new tools may come on the scene that were not even invented when we wrote this. That's why you want to regularly visit our website, http://KloutMatters. com, and our Facebook page about some of the latest announcements.

The tools listed here can help you to operate your social media business much more easily. These tools can help you to grow and build your community, at the same time enhancing your influence in the blogsphere and social media world. We look forward to your comments.

Resource	Where to Find It	Comments
Photo Pin	http://photopin. com	Get royalty-free pictures for your website. Be sure to reference them—that's all Photo Pin asks, and it is the right thing to do.
Eyejot	www.eyejot.com	This tool helps you to send a video e-mail without you or your recipient needing to load a bunch of software. Very nice.
BottleNose	http://bottlenose. com/#folders/main	Tool for organizing your social media channels and life. Think of it like an executive dashboard for your social media needs.
Smartr	https://www.xobni. com/download/ gmail	Organize your Gmail, social media networks, and more with this handy tool. We are blown away by the capabilities it has to help you stay in touch with people and engage.

Resource	Where to Find It	Comments
BossJock	http://bossjock studio.com	Create podcasts on your smart-phone, iPad, or tablet and send them to the world. Get into pod-casting now with this tool.
Test your read-ing speed	http://www. staples.com/sbd/ cre/marketing/tech-nology-research-centers/ereaders/ speed-reader/index. html	We love this tool. Find out what your reading speed is and your level of comprehension. From Staples, this is a great resource to test yourself and get the necessary motivation to improve.
Audacity	http://audacity. sourceforge.net	This is a great audio-editing tool that is open source and free. It can do a great job editing your audio podcasts, and it is some-thing for every thought leader to examine.
SpeakPipe	www.SpeakPipe. com	This plug-in allows visitors to your website to leave an audio comment for you. This can be particularly helpful in audio pod-casts to get real feedback from your listeners.
Survey Monkey	www. SurveyMonkey. com	Content creators alert! Rather than trying to think what you believe is important for your market, ask community members. Survey monkey is a great tool for this.
Video Conferencing with Google+ Hangout	https://tools. google.com/dlpage/ hangoutplugin	This is a great way to have a free video conference with up to 10 people. For learning, promotion, and connecting, you can't beat it.
Video Conferencing with Skype	www.Skype.com	Since Skype was a client of Terry's—and he remains a big fan—we have to mention this. Leverage the power of Skype to reach people worldwide.
Buffer	https://bufferapp. com	Tool for automatic scheduling of social news you send.

Resource	Where to Find It	Comments
Rapportive	www.Rapportive.com	Used with Gmail to identify various ways on social media and more to reach your contacts. Good for building relationships.
Social Mention	www.social mention.com	Like Google Alert, but for social media. Find what the social media world is saying about a topic, a trend, or yourself!
Gina's Tips on Boosting Your Klout Score	http://Klout Matters.com/ KloutTips	Some handy tips that can help you boost your Klout Score by doing some simple exercises.

Notes

Introduction

1. Gina Carr, "Klout Scores Big with 400 Signals," Technorati, http://technorati.com/social-media/article/klout-scores-big-with-400-signals.
2. From Klout web page, http://klout.com/#/corp/klout_score.
3. Seth Stevenson, "What your Klout Score Really Means," *Wired* magazine, April 24, 2012, http://www.wired.com/business/2012/04/ff_klout.
4. John Heilpern, "Silver Streak: The Political-Forecasting Phenom Has a New Book—and an Election Bet," *Vanity Fair*, November 2012, http://www.vanityfair.com/politics/2012/11/nate-silver-mitt-romney-has-one-in-three-chance.
5. Eric Kuhn and David Tochterman, "A Digital Agent Walks into a Panel . . ." (panel discussion, New Media Expo, Las Vegas, NV, January 6, 2013).
6. Jeff Bullas, "Does Thought Leadership Need Social Media?" (blog), http://www.jeffbullas.com/2013/02/05/does-thought-leadership-need-social-media.
7. Mari Smith, Klout Matters Expert Contributor Survey, http://.MariSmith.com, from personal note to the authors, March 31, 2013.
8. David Perlmutter, "Journalism 101 for Bloggers" (presentation at New Media Expo, Las Vegas, NV, January 7, 2013).

Chapter 1

1. "Healthy Weight—It's Not a Diet, It's a Lifestyle!" (blog post), Centers for Disease Control, http://www.cdc.gov/healthyweight/index.html.
2. Randy Gage, video interview with Terry Brock for this book, March 12, 2013, http://www.KloutMatters.com/videos-and-more.
3. Ibid.
4. Bob Burg, video interview with Terry Brock for this book, March 11, 2013, http://www.KloutMatters.com/videos-and-more.

Chapter 2

1. Menachem Wecker, "Professor Sparks Controversy for Klout-Based Grading," *US News & World Report*, August 29, 2012, http://www.

usnews.com/education/best-colleges/articles/2012/08/29/professor-sparks-controversy-for-klout-based-grading.

2. Ryan Thornburg, "Klout in the Classroom: Grading Students on Social Media Use," PBS Idea Lab, October 9, 2012, http://www.pbs.org/idealab/2012/10/klout-in-the-classroom-grading-students-on-social-media-use281.html.

3. "Bizarre Trend: Journalism Professors Using Klout Scores as Part of Students' Grades," Techdirt (blog), http://www.techdirt.com/articles/20121020/01463320773/bizarre-trend-journalism-professors-using-klout-scores-as-part-students-grades.shtml.

4. Alan Stevens, Klout Matters Expert Contributor Survey, March 2013.

Chapter 3

1. Alan Stevens, video interview with Terry Brock for this book, March 10, 2013, http://www.KloutMatters.com/videos-and-more.

Chapter 4

1. Kevin Allen, "Social Media Influences Consumer's Purchasing Decisions: Study," Ragan's PR Daily, February 18, 2013, http://www.prdaily.com/Main/Articles/Social_media_influences_consumers_purchasing_decis_13855.aspx.

Chapter 5

1. Craig Duswalt, "How to Create New Content and Think Outside the Box When Podcasting" (presentation at New Media Expo, Las Vegas, NV, January 7, 2013).

2. Kathryn Rose, Klout Matters Expert Contributor Survey, March 1, 2013.

3. Brian Tracy, *Getting Rich in America* (audio learning program), http://www.nightingale.com/prod_detail~product~Getting_Rich_America.aspx.

4. Kim Garst, "Top 3 Social Media Mistakes Made by Small Businesses," Boom! Social, October 15, 2012, http://kimgarst.com/top-3-social-media-mistakes-made-by-small-businesses.

5. Kim Garst, video interview with Terry Brock for this book, March 12, 2013, http://KloutMatters.com/videos-and-more.

6. Edel O'Mahoney, Klout Matters Expert Contributor Survey, March 2013.

7. Kim LaChance Shandrow, "What You Can Learn from Justin Bieber About Marketing on Twitter," *Entrepreneur* magazine, March 4, 2013, http://www.entrepreneur.com/article/225979.

Chapter 6

1. Aaron Lee, "6 Unofficial Ways to Increase Your Klout Score," Ask Aaron Lee, http://askaaronlee.com/increase-klout-score.
2. Kare Anderson, video interview with Terry Brock for this book, March 12, 2013, http://KloutMatters.com/videos-and-more.

Chapter 7

1. John Scalzi, "Why Klout Scores Are Possibly Evil," CNNMoney, November 15, 2011, http://money.cnn.com/2011/11/15/technology/klout_scores/index.htm.
2. "Does My Klout Score Suck, or Does Klout?," The Digital Drew (blog), January 27, 2013, http://thedigitaldrew.com/tag/klout-score.
3. Scott Levy, "Klout vs. Kred: Which, If Any, Is Better for Your Business?" (blog), March 4, 2013, http://forbes.com/sites/scottlevy/2013/03/04/klout-vs-kred-which-if-any-is-better-for-your-business/?commentId=comment_blogAndPostId/blog/comment/2501-76-12.
4. Mark Fidelman, video interview with Terry Brock for this book, March 12, 2013, http://KloutMatters.com/videos-and-more.
5. Joe Fernandez, personal interview with Terry Brock and Gina Carr for this book, March 4, 2013, at Klout headquarters, San Francisco, California.
6. Ibid.
7. Genesys website, http://ow.ly/kxNZ2.
8. Patrick Thomas, "Cirque du Soleil Sends 50 Klout Users to Exclusive SxSW Interactive Event" (blog), February 28, 2013, http://corp.klout.com/blog/2013/02/cirque-du-soleil-and-klout.
9. Mark W. Schaefer, personal interview with Terry Brock and Gina Carr for this book (phone conversation), January 4, 2013.
10. Jon Dick, personal interview with Terry Brock and Gina Carr, March 4, 2013, at Klout headquarters, San Francisco, California.
11. Debbie Horovitch, Klout Matters Expert Contributor Survey.
12. Jon Dick, personal interview with Terry Brock and Gina Carr, March 4, 2013, at Klout Headquarters, San Francisco, California.
13. Natt Garun, "Klout Offers 'Real Life Perks' by Granting VIP Access to Los Angeles Nightclub," August 9, 2012, http://www.digitaltrends.com/lifestyle/klout-real-life-perks/#ixzz2O06xbacG.
14. Matthew Thomson, "Influence Data for the Stars from Crimson Hexagon" (the official Klout blog), December 12, 2012, http://corp.klout.com/blog/2012/12/influence-data-for-the-stars-from-crimson-hexagon.
15. "About TREMOR" (blog), http://www.tremor.com/about-us.

16. Michelle Colon-Johnson, post on "Klout Matters" private Facebook Group, February 2013.

17. Carly Alyssa Thorne, Klout Matters Expert Contributor Survey, March 6, 2013.

18. "Consumer Trust in Online, Social and Mobile Advertising Grows," Nielsen, April 10, 2012, http://www.nielsen.com/us/en/newswire/ 2012/consumer-trust-in-online-social-and-mobile-advertising-grows. html.

Chapter 8

1. Alexandra Samuel, "How to Make Space for Social Media" (blog post), *Harvard Business Review*, March 6, 2013, http://blogs.hbr.org/ samuel/2013/03/how-to-make-space-for-social-m.html.

2. Miriam Slozberg, private e-mail message to authors, March 7, 2013.

3. J. B. Glossinger, video interview with Terry Brock for this book, March 12, 2013, http://kloutmatters.com/videos-and-more.

4. Lisa Jimenez, video interview with Terry Brock for this book, March 12, 2013, http://www.kloutmatters.com/videos-and-more.

5. Gina Rau, comment posted on Quora, June 17, 2011, http://www. quora.com/EdgeRank/Does-Facebook-EdgeRank-give-lower- significance-to-posts-from-3rd-party-tools-such-as-HootSuite- SocialOomph-or-TweetDeck.

6. Srinivas Rao, Klout Matters Expert Contributor Survey, March 8, 2013.

7. Jeffrey Hayzlett, Klout Matters Expert Contributor Survey, March 6, 2013.

8. Andrea Vahl, Klout Matters Expert Contributor Survey, March 7, 2013.

9. The Build Network, blog post from unknown date, http:// thebuildnetwork.com/leadership/management/peter-drucker- patron-saint.

10. Paul Kim, private interview with the authors, March 4, 2013, Klout headquarters, San Francisco, California.

Chapter 10

1. Winston Marsh, private interview with the authors over Skype, February 28, 2013.

2. Robert Scoble, "Icons and Influencers" (panel discussion), New Media Expo, Las Vegas, NV, January 2013.

3. Mitch Joel, "Icons and Influencers" (panel discussion), New Media Expo, Las Vegas, NV, January 2013.

4. Joe Fernandez, private interview with the authors, March 4, 2013, at Klout headquarters, San Francisco, CA.

5. Mary Kelly, Klout Matters Expert Contributor Survey, February 27, 2013.
6. Alan Stevens, Klout Matters Expert Contributor Survey, February 26, 2013.
7. Sahana Ullagaddi, private interview with the authors, March 4, 2013, at Klout headquarters, San Francisco, CA.

Chapter 11

1. Joe Fernandez, private interview with the authors, March 4, 2013, Klout headquarters, San Francisco, CA.
2. "The Klout Score," http://klout.com/#/corp/klout_score.

Chapter 12

1. Kathryn Rose, Klout Matters Expert Contributor Survey, March 1, 2013.
2. "Klout Score," http://klout.com/#/corp/klout_score.
3. Kim Garst, Klout Matters Expert Contributor Survey, March 2013.
4. Jay Baer, "Solving Klout's Warren Buffett Problem," Convince & Convert, March 2013, http://convinceandconvert.com/social-pros-podcast/solving-klouts-warren-buffett-problem.
5. Gina Schreck, Klout Matters Expert Contributor Survey, March 2013.
6. Ibid.
7. Kim Garst, Klout Matters Expert Contributor Survey, March 2013.
8. Ibid.

Chapter 13

1. Andrea Vahl, Klout Matters Expert Contributor Survey, March 2013.
2. Mari Smith, Klout Matters Expert Contributor Survey, March 2013.
3. Miriam Slozberg, "How Klout Score Is Calculated," June 2013, http://dashburst.com/how-klout-score-is-calculated/.

Chapter 14

1. Klout Score—Corporate, http://klout.com/#/corp/klout_score.
2. http://klout.com/#/corp/klout_score.
3. Expert tip by Heather Lutze, speaker and author of *The Findability Formula: The Easy Nontechnical Approach to Search Engine Marketing* and *Thumbonomics: The Essential Business Roadmap for Social Media and Mobile Marketing*.

Chapter 15

1. Ding Zhou, private interview with the authors, March 4, 2013, Klout headquarters, San Francisco. Zhou explained that the August 2012 revamp of the Klout algorithm was internally known as Maxwell, named after the famed physicist James Clerk Maxwell (http://en.wikipedia. org/wiki/James_Clerk_Maxwell).
2. Klout Score—Corporate, http://klout.com/#/corp/klout_score.
3. Dianna Booher, private e-mail with the authors.
4. Joe Fernandez, Expand Your Influence with Klout Experts, May 8, 2013, http://corp.klout.com/blog/2013/05/klout-experts/#sthash. 9xxjgOOA.w8mhQZkI.dpuf.
5. Joel Comm, Klout Matters Expert Contributor Survey, May 2013.

Chapter 16

1. http://en.wikipedia.org/wiki/Reciprocity_(social_and_political_ philosophy).
2. Robert Cialdini, *Influence: Science and Practice*, http://en.wikipedia. org/wiki/Influence_Science_and_Practice.
3. Laura Rubinstein, Klout Matters Expert Contributor Survey, March 2013.
4. Dwayne Kilbourne, Klout Matters Expert Contributor Survey, February 2013.

Chapter 18

1. Read more at http://www.brainyquote.com/quotes/quotes/j/ jimrohn147491.html#lsQjJobGPw7MaQfQ.99.
2. Ding Zhou, private interview with the authors, March 4, 2013, Klout headquarters, San Francisco.
3. Ibid.

Chapter 19

1. Mari Smith is a premier Facebook marketing expert, author of *The New Relationship Marketing*, and coauthor of *Facebook Marketing: An Hour a Day*.

Chapter 20

1. *New York Times* bestselling author of *Twitter Power and Kaching*.

Index

Achievement Systems, Inc., 71
Action:
  motivating others to take, 5, 13
  taking positive, 189
  as tangible thing, 36
Advice, posting, 135
Advocate marketing, 3–4, 60, 61, 66
Algorithm(s), 1, 6, 13
  getting a true picture of influence
    through, 57
  Klout Score as series of, 33
  Maxwell, 153
Amazon, 96
American Institute of Certified Public
    Accountants (AICPA), 184
Amyporterfield.com, 199
Analysis, quantitative, 2, 6–9
Anderson, Kare, 47
Appinions, 6, 8, 53
Apple, 109
Arbitron, 44
Archaeologists, 21
@ mentions, 35, 127–130
Attention, 109
  competition for, 34–35
  focusing your, 175–176
  getting, 180
AT&T's Networking Exchange Blog, 94
Audacity (audio-editing tool), 88, 203
Authority, positioning yourself as an, 183

Bacile, Todd, 22
Baer, Jay, 127–128, 201
*Beware the Naked Man Who Offers
    You His Shirt* (Mackay), 77, 102
Bieber, Justin, 39, 44
Big data, 6–8, 59
Bing, 8–9, 54, 55, 60, 155–157
The Black Eyed Peas, 123
Blain, Amanda, 157–158
Blip.tv, 172
Blogcast.fm (podcast), 21, 81
Blogger (app), 95

Bloggers, 61–62
Blogs, 83–84
  as fundamental element of intellectual
    diet, 197
  and Klout Score, 173–174
  recommended, 196–201
Body-mass index (BMI), 15–17, 37
Bones (Triberr), 160
Booher, Dianna, 138–139
Boom! Social, 37
BossJock, 203
BottleNose, 203
Brands, 3, 63–65
  and connecting with key influencers,
    59
  and perks, 59–61
  and quantitative analysis, 192
Brenner, Michael, 99
Broadcasters, 26
Broadcasting, 65
Brock, Terry, 39, 67, 198
Brogan, Chris, 56, 199
Browne, Harry, 182–183
B2B Marketing, 200
BufferApp, 95–96, 204
The Build Network (blog), 87
Building community, 75
Bullas, Jeff, 10, 198
Burg, Bob, 19, 142, 200
Burg.com, 200
Business, 31–32
Business building, resources for,
    202–204
Business connections, and LinkedIn, 147
Business success, 37
Business-building tips, 71–91
  being a resource for others, 80–83
  building a team, 86–90
  committing to social media, 77–80
  continuing to learn and grow, 84–85
  defining your purpose, 72–74
  engaging with communities, 85–86
  expanding your network, 90

focusing on specific niche, 90–91
providing a unique point of view,
  83–85
selecting platforms, 74–77
Businessgrow.com, 198
Buyers, 21, 74–75
Buying decisions, and Klout Score(s),
  54–55
Buzzwords, 1

Caldini, Robert B., 159
Call to action (Facebook), 141
Carmen, Sandy Weaver, 51
Carr, Gina, 198
"Cat's-paw marketing," 66
Celebrities:
  influence factor of, 189–190
  interacting with, 180–181, 183, 186
Chat rooms, 126
Chevy Volt, 59
Chrisbrogan.com, 199
Cirque du Soleil, 61
Citizens, social media, 39
Classic podcasts, listening to, 176
Click to Tweet, 127
Clout, 10
CNBC.com, 43
CNET.com, 109
CNN.com, 43
CNNMoney (blog), 53
Colon-Johnson, Michelle, 66
Comm, Joel, 156–157, 189
Comments:
  on Facebook, 134
  as signal of influence, on LinkedIn,
    147
Communication(s), 10
  adding audio and video to, 81–82
  public, 112–113
  as two-way street, 26
Community(-ies), 74–75
  building, 168
  enabling others in your, 75–76
  engaging with, 85–86
  engaging/nurturing your, 104–105
  responsive, 35
Compelling content:
  creating, 33–34, 41, 79
  focusing on creating, 45–46
  providing, 44

Competence:
  demonstrating, 184
  in your niche, 90
Competitive advantage:
  with blogs, 196
  gaining, through YouTube/podcasts/
    blogs, 177
  quality content and, 36
  with YouTube, 195
Compliments (on Facebook), 142
Conferences:
  attending live, benefits of, 78, 84
  YouTube videos of, 195
Connections, as signal of influence on
  LinkedIn, 147
Consistency, 36, 111–112
Consumer advocacy, 65
Content, 32
  creating, 17–18, 25–27, 87–88,
    114–115
  promoting, 87
  providing valuable, 184–185
Content Marketing Blog, 201
Contextual references, 9
Controversial topics, avoiding, 102
Conversations:
  engaging with communities through,
    86
  Twitter as main driver of, 123
Convinceandconvert.com, 201
CopyBlogger, 200
Credentials, education, 151
Credibility:
  building, 56, 181–182
  street, 81
Critical thinking, 22, 190
Criticisms of Klout, 52–54, 57–59
Curation, of information, 82
Current, remaining, 185
Current events, posting, 143
Customers:
  engaging with, 16
  needs and wants of, 62

Data:
  big, 6–8, 59
  reliable, 2
Decision makers, 7
Definiteness of purpose, 72
DeGeneres, Ellen, 44

Democratization of ideas, 180
Description, changing, 120–121
Dialog, engaging in, 26
Dick, Jon, 61, 64
The Digital Drew (blog), 56
Digital influence:
  assigning a score to, 39
  increasing your, 4
  measurement of, 6
Digital Trends, 64
Digital world, "real-life activities" vs.,
  186
Discipline:
  required for serious social media
    work, 89
  required for "University of You," 177
Discussions, virtual, 126
Dostoevsky, Fyodor, 46
Drucker, Peter, 79, 87, 89
Dungy, Tony, 69, 83
Duswalt, Craig, 34–35

Eastman Kodak, 148
Edge Rank, 96, 145
Editing (outsourcing of), 88–89
Educational materials, in audio format,
  193
Effectiveness, marketing, 37
Elance, 79, 89
Empire Avenue (EAv), 161–162
Employment decisions, and Klout
  Scores, 29
Enabling others, 75–76
Endless Referrals (Burg), 19
Engagement, 10, 114, 179
  with customers, 16, 44, 47
  increasing, 27, 148
  with others (*see* Interacting with
    others)
  as personal requirement for social
    media, 79
  and social media, 146
Enhancing your social media presence,
  99–115
  by always providing value first,
    109–111
  by becoming a "go to" person, 106
  by being consistent, 111–112
  by being fast in a niche market,
    108–109

by creating "scrap time" blocks,
  113–114
by engaging/nurturing your
  community, 104–105
by feeding your beast, 107
by having fun, 111
by knowing your visitors, 101–102
by not focusing on boosting your
  Klout Score, 114–115
by providing valuable information,
  100
by sharing ideas from others, 108
by solving problems, 103–104
by staying connected, 105–106
by talking about important events,
  101
by telling/sharing stories, 100,
  107–108
by using social media for
  communication, 112–113
by visiting other sites in your
  community, 101
Entrepreneur magazine, 39
Ethics, of online collaboration groups,
  163
Evernote, 95
"The Evolution of Dance" (video),
  171–172
Evolve (company), 58
Experimentation, in selecting
  communities/tribes, 75–77
Expert, becoming an, 183–186
Expertise, influence determined
  through, 57
Eyejot, 80, 96–97, 203

Facebook, 14, 36, 95
  buying friends on, 166
  connecting to Klout account with,
    117
  groups on, 162
  Personal Profile on, 118
  raising your Klout Score with,
    133–146
  requesting public comments on,
    112–113
*Facebook Marketing All-in-One for
  Dummies* (Vahl, Porterfield, and
  Khare), 86
Facebook Page, 118

Facilitating, 10
Fan base, building, 109–110
Feedback:
  podcasts as tools for, 174
  from surveys, 110
Feedly, 96
Fernandez, Joe, 1, 3, 16, 19, 37
  on connecting accounts on Klout, 119
  on consistency with social media, 111–112
  on Google, 59
  on hiring with Klout, 58
  on Klout Experts, 156
  on YouTube/podcasts/blogs, 173
FICO scores, 15, 17
Fidelman, Mark, 58
Fiorella, Sam, 4
Flint River Ranch, 51
Flipboard, 108
Florida State University, 22
Follow Friday Tweets (#FF), 129
"Follow the money," 15
Followers, raising your Klout Score with, 131
Forbes magazine, 47, 57, 58
Foxnews.com, 43
Freedomain Radio, 173
FreedomFest, 182
Freelancer.com, 89
Fritz, Marshall, 183

Gage, Randy, 19, 60, 135, 200
Gaming the system, 18–19, 41–49, 55
  by buying Twitter followers, 45–46
  by doing the +K gig, 46–47
  and online collaborative networks, 159
  by using "like" farms, 43–45
  and your reputation, 48–49
Gangnam Style, 171
Garee, Jane, 141
Garst, Kim, 37–38, 131–132, 140–141
Garun, Natt, 64
Genesys, 60
Getting Rich in America (audio series), 36–37
Getting started with Klout, 117–122
Gigaom, 199
GinaCarr.com, 198
Gina's Tips on Boosting Your Klout Score, 204

Gitomer, Jeffrey, 33
Gizmodo.com, 108
Global brand, 31
Global individuals, thought leaders as, 30
Global Trust in Advertising (report), 66
Glossinger, J. B., 76
Gmail, 95
Godin, Seth, 25, 63, 201
The Go-Giver (Burg and Mann), 19
Google, 5, 9, 18, 43, 60
Google+, raising your Klout Score with, 157–158
Google Alerts, 105–106
Google+ Hangouts, 80, 110–111, 204
Graphs, with TweetBinder, 98
Grill, Andrew, 16
Group interactions, in Facebook, 134
Groups, online collaborative (*see* Online collaborative networks [OCNs])

Harris, Sharon, 183
Harvard Business Review, 70
Harvard Business School, 22
Hashtags, 97, 125–127
Hayek, Friedrich, 126
Hayzlett, Jeffrey, 85, 143, 148, 150–151
Hill, Napoleon, 72
Hoffman, Reid, 147
Hootlet, 94, 97
HootSuite, 60, 94–95, 97
Horovitch, Debbie, 62
Huffington Post, 47
Humor, posting to Facebook, 138

Ideas:
  listening to current, 176
  sharing, 108
Influence:
  and being retweeted, 5
  digital, 39
  general, 191
  grading/rating, 1
  level of, 33
  long-term, 20
  maintaining, 47
  measuring, 2–3, 37, 190–191
  and persuasiveness, 189–192
  and searches, 9

specific, 191
Influence: Science and Practice
   (Caldini), 159
Influence factor, of celebrities,
   189–190
Influencers:
   choosing, 120
   marketing via key, 6
   reaching, 52
   reaching out to, 131
Influential factors, offline, 9
Influential persons, 21
Information:
   accumulation of, 8
   being hub of, 82
   collecting, with Mackay 66 tool,
      102–103
   curators of, 168
   paying for, 168–169
   providing valuable, 100
Informative posts, writing, 138
Inlinks, number of, on Wikipedia, 154
Insincere flattery, genuine praise vs., 47
Inspirational posts, on Facebook, 139
Instagram, 95, 156–157
Intellectual diet:
   blogs as fundamental element of, 197
   YouTube as part of, 194
Interacting with others, 179–187
   and becoming an expert, 183–186
   and building credibility, 181–182
   celebrities, 180–181, 183, 186
   as focus of Klout, 179
   and getting attention, 180
   and Klout Score, 179
   preparing for, 182–183
Interaction, positive, 183
Interests, posting about, 135

Jackson Memorial Hospital, 16
Jeffbullas.com, 198
Jimenez, Lisa, 78, 81, 200
Job experience, 9
Job requirements, 23
Jobs, Steve, 93
Joel, Mitch, 107, 199
Journalists, 14–15
Judgment, in selecting communities/
   tribes, 75

+Ks, 8, 46–47
Kelly, Mary, 112
Key influencers, 31, 66, 102–103
Kilbourne, Dwayne, 162
Klout:
   and Bing search engine, 54–55
   as connecting point between vendors
      and Klout users, 63
   criticisms of, 52–54, 57–59
   focus of, 179
   getting started with, 117–122
   legitimacy of, 53
   signing up for, 117–122
   users of, 21–23
   as work-in-progress, 59
Klout algorithm, 171
Klout Experts, 156
Klout Moments, 145
Klout Score(s), 7, 13–20
   actions not contributing to your,
      171–177
   balanced approach to, 55–58
   and blogs, 101
   blogs and, 173–174
   BMI vs., 15–16
   building with sound business policies,
      49
   criticism of, 15
   enhancing by building an audience, 42
   focusing on, 16
   frustration with, 17
   importance of, 29–32
   integration of, into customer service
      platforms, 60
   and interaction with others, 179
   key to increasing your, 83
   link system of, 167–168
   and making buying decisions, 54–55
   obsession with, 169
   podcasts and, 174–177
   related to business bottom line, 114
   searches and, 9
   YouTube videos and, 171–173
   (*See also* Raising your Klout Score)
"Kloutlaws," 58–59
Kred, 6, 8, 53, 57
Kuhn, Eric, 7–8

Laipply, Judson, 172
Laissez Faire Book Club, 199

Leaders, thought, 10, 25
Learning, 186
  lifelong, 72
  online, 84–85
Lee, Aaron, 41–42
Legitimacy (of Klout), 53
Levy, Scott, 57–58
Lewis, Benny, 69
Libertarian party, 182
Life, posting about, 137
Lifelong learning, 72
"Like" farms, using, 43–45
Likes, in Facebook, 134
Link farms, 41, 43
LinkedIn, 95, 103
  business connections and, 147
  raising your Klout Score with, 147–151
Listorious, 123
Lists, raising your Klout Score with,
  130–131
The Little Red Book of Selling
  (Gitomer), 33
Local business, 30–31
Long-term influence, 20
Lutze, Heather, 152

Mackay, Harvey, 77, 102–103
Mackay 66 tool, 102–103
Managing social media, 93–98
Marcandangel.com, 201
Marismith.com, 199
Marketing, 26, 79
  advocate, 3–4, 60, 61
  effectiveness of, 37
  focusing on credibility in, 48
  multilevel, 48
  to a niche, 42
  permission-based, 63
  "spray and pray," 3, 61–62
  via key influencers, 6
  viral, 45
  your presence on social media, 87
Marketing tricks, ninja, 109
Marksanborn.com, 200
Marsh, Winston, 106, 107, 135–136
Mashable, 199
Mass communication advertising, 65
Maxwell algorithm, 153
Measurement:
  gut feelings vs., 2

social media, 34
The Media Coach (blog), 25, 197
Meetings, attending live, 78
Mentions:
  @ (Twitter), 35, 127–130
  on Facebook, 133–134
Messages:
  communicating, with stories, 107–108
  creating relevant, 104
  viral, 85
Microsoft, 8–9, 54, 55
The Millionaire Next Door (Stanley
  and Danko), 82, 106
Missions (Empire Avenue), 162
Mobile marketing, 63
Molyneux, Stefan, 173
Morning Coach (podcast), 76
MSNBC.com, 43
Muck Rack, 123
Multilevel marketing, 48
Myths, about raising your Klout Score,
  165–169

National Speakers Association, 74, 77
Network, expanding your, 90
Networking Exchange Blog, 94, 201
New Media Expo, 7
New York Times, 9, 43, 60, 77, 102, 156
Niche, focusing on a specific, 90–91
Nielsen Ratings, 37, 44, 66
Nightingale, Earl, 185–186
Ninja marketing tricks, 109
Ninja-level social media effectiveness
  guide, 114–115
Ninjas, social media, 104–105
"Nose for News," 107
Nurturance, of community members,
  105

Obama, Barack, 44
Objective process, 8
OCNs (*see* Online collaborative
  networks)
oDesk.com, 79, 89
Offline influence, measurement of, 2, 9,
  151, 153
Offline influential factors, 9
O'Mahony, Edel, 38
Online collaborative networks (OCNs),
  159–163

Empire Avenue, 161–162
  ethics of, 163
  Facebook groups, 162
  factors in choosing, 163
  Social Buzz Club, 160–161
  Triberr, 160
Online consumer reviews, 66
Online influence, measurement of, 2
Online learning, 84–85
Online presence, examining visitors',
  101–102
Opt-in system, 63
Outlinks, ratio of inlinks to, on
  Wikipedia, 154

Page importance, on Wikipedia,
  154
PageRank, 154
Participation, active, 22–23
Patrick, Danica, 51
PeerIndex, 6, 8
Perera, Gihan, 106
Perks, 59–67, 109–110
  and authenticity, 66–67
  and brand development, 59–65
  discussion of, 64
  and marketing, 62–63
Perlmutter, David, 12
Permission-based marketing, 63
Personal contact, 79–80
Persuasiveness, 189–192
Photo Pin, 202
Pictures, posting on Facebook, 144
Platforms:
  finding, 115
  selecting, 74–77
Podcasts:
  and Klout Score, 174–177
  recommended, 193
Point of view, 83–85
Portable technology, 104
Porterfield, Amy, 199
Positive interaction, to tweets, 183
Post Planner, 96
PowerIndex, 53
Praise, insincere flattery vs., 47
Preparation, 182–183
Problems, solving, 103–104
ProBlogger, 200
Procter & Gamble, 64–65

Professional organizations, as
  community, 74
Promotion, 56, 111
Prosperity Blog, Randy Gage's, 200
Public communication(s), 112–113
Public speaking, 9
Pulizzi, Joe, 201
Purpose, defining, 72–74

Quantitative analysis, 2, 6–9, 192
Quantitative results, 34
Questions, 135
Quick fixes, avoiding, 48
Quora, 78

Radio, as root of podcasting, 174
Ragan's PR Daily (news site), 31–32
Raising your Klout Score, 17–19,
  123–158
  with Bing, 155–157
  with Facebook, 133–146
  with Google+, 157–158
  with LinkedIn, 147–151
  managing social media and, 93–98
  myths about, 165–169
  with Twitter, 123–132
  value of, 33–39
  with Wikipedia, 153–155
Rao, Srinivas, 21, 81
Rapportive, 95, 204
Rau, Gina, 78–79
Rayburn, Mike, 197
R-commerce (relationships), 49
Reciprocity, 159, 162
Recommenders, as signal of influence
  on LinkedIn, 147
References, 9, 35
Relationships, developing, 7
Relevance, creating messages with, 104
Reliable data, 2
Reputation, and gaming the system,
  48–49
Resource, being a, 80–83
Respect, building genuine, 181
Responsive community, social media
  as, 35
Results, quantitative, 34
Return on Influence (Schaefer), 29, 61
Retweets:
  action resulting from, 5–6

as actions taken in response to posts,
    35–36
effect of, on score, 3
raising your Klout Score with, 124–
    125
Reynolds, Kimberly, 32
Rich Media, 148, 150
Risks, taking, 60
Risky Is the New Safe (Gage), 60
Rohn, Jim, 171
Rose, Kathryn, 35, 123, 160
RSS feeds, 160
Rubinstein, Laura, 160–161
Rx-success.com, 200

The Sales Lion, 198
Samuels, Alexandra, 70
Sanborn, Mark, 200
Sandberg, Sheryl, 133
Sandboxing, 43
SAP, 99
Scalzi, John, 53
Schaefer, Mark W., 29, 43, 61, 198
Scheduling tools, 95–96
Schreck, Gina, 130–131, 138, 157
Scoble, Robert, 107
Scoring companies, social media
    influence, 4
Scoring system, social, 2
Scrap time, 113–114
Search engine optimization (SEO), 18,
    43, 167
Search engines, 8, 194–195
Search engine/social scoring integration,
    54, 55
Searches, as component of influence, 9
SEO (search engine optimization), 18
Sethgodin.typepad.com, 201
Silver, Nate, 6
Six Pixels of Separation, 199
Skousen, Mark, 182–183
Skype, 80, 111, 204
Smartphones, 63, 175
Smartr, 203
Smith, Mari, 10, 30, 144, 179, 199
Social Buzz Club, 123, 160–161
Social equity, using engagement to
    build, 10
Social experience, 34
Social influence, 2, 63

Social media, 1–2, 10
    and access to distribution, 16
    building success in, 78
    committing to, 77–80
    communicating with, 112–113
    constant changes in, 4
    and consumers, 51–52
    effectiveness, Klout Scores as
        measurement of, 29
    emphasis on "social" in, 100
    enhancing your presence on (*see*
        Enhancing your social media
        presence)
    finding time for, 69–71
    leveraging, with portable technology,
        104
    managing, 93–98
    marketing your presence on, 87–88
    putting quality time into, 77
    and relationships, 35
    revolution of, 52
    streams in, 94
    success, 23
    as term, 19
    and time commitment, 25–26
    as tool, 76
Social media citizens, 39
Social media concierge, 62
Social media effectiveness guide, ninja-
    level, 114–115
Social Media Examiner, 198
Social media influence scoring
    companies, 4
Social media marketing, as profession,
    38
Social media measurement, 34
Social media ninjas, 104–105
Social Media Partners, 162
Social media success, 23
Social Mention, 204
Social scoring systems, 2
Social scoring/search engine integration,
    54, 55
Socialized! (Fidelman), 58
Solution(s):
    becoming the, 182
    for customers, 192
Solving the Social Media Puzzle (Rose),
    123
Solzberg, Miriam, 75

South by Southwest (SXSW), 61
Speak Pipe, 110, 204
"Spray and pray" marketing, 3, 61–63
Stanley, Tom, 82–83, 106
Stevens, Alan, 23, 25–26, 113–114, 197
Stories:
  communicating your message with,
    107–108
  telling, 100
Street credibility (street cred), 81
Subcontractors, 86
Success, 4–5
  business, 37
  principles of, 73–74
  social media, 23, 78
Success Blog (Lisa Jimenez), 200
Sugarman, Joe, 26–27
Survey Monkey, 110, 204
Survey results, collecting, 110
*Swim with the Sharks Without Being
  Eaten Alive* (Mackay), 77, 102
SXSW (South by Southwest), 61

Tags, in Facebook, 134
The Tao of Twitter (Schaefer), 29
Targeting, as effective advertising, 61
Tasks, as "beast," 107
Team, building a, 86–90
Techcrunch, 200
Technology, leveraging, 110
TerryBrock.com, 198
Test your reading speed (online tool),
  203
Think and Grow (Hill), 72
Thomson, Matt, 127–128
Thornburg, Ryan, 22
Thorne, Carly Alyssa, 66
Thought leaders, 10, 25
  competency of, 72
  and competition for attention, 34–35
  demand for skills of, 72–73
  expendability of, 73
  as global individuals, 30
  judgment of, 54–55
  time constraints on, 70
Thought-provoking posts, on Facebook,
  141
Time:
  monopolizing, 180
  as resource, 176

Time Management for Social Media
  (program), 71
Title, as signal of influence on LinkedIn,
  147
Tochterman, David, 7
Todaymade, 127
Tools, raising your Klout Score with, 132
Topics:
  adjusting, 119–120
  choosing, 118
Tracy, Brian, 36–37
Tran, Binh, 3
TREMOR™, 65
Triberr, 160
Tribes, 74 (*See also* Community[-ies])
Trust:
  in advertisements, 109
  building, 27
Trusted advisor, positioning yourself
  as, 80
Tumblr, 95, 173–174
Turkel, Bruce, 15–16
Tweet Embed, 127
Tweet streams, 130
Tweet This, 127–128
TweetBinder, 98
TweetChats, 126, 130–131
Tweets, 3, 129
Twellow, 123
Twistimage.com, 199
Twitter, 14, 36, 95
  account, visible to public, 30
  connecting to Klout account with,
    117
  raising your Klout Score with,
    123–132
  requesting public comments on,
    112–113
  rude/inappropriate content, 38
  (*See also* Retweets)
Twitter followers, buying, 45–46,
  165–166
Twitter handles, as podcast tools, 174
21.5 Unbreakable Laws of Selling
  (Gitomer), 33
Twubs, 97, 126

Ullagaddi, Sahana, 114
University of Iowa, 12
"University of You," 177

Unsustainability, of "gaming the system," 42–43
URL shortener, 94
Users, of Klout, 21–23

Vahl, Andrea, 86, 137
Validity, of scoring system for influence, 55
Value:
  providing, 99, 109
  of raising your Klout Score, 33–39
  as requirement, for interaction/ engagement, 181
Variety, 137–138
Video, as tool for creating connections, 80
Videoconferencing, 110
Vimeo, 172
Viral marketing, 45
Viral messages, 85
Virgin America, 59
Virtual assistants, 86
Virtual discussions, 126
Visitors, knowing your, 101–102
Voice mail responses, as podcast tools, 174
Von Rosen, Viveka, 148–150

Wall posts, on Facebook, 134
Wall Street Journal, 142
Website feedback, as podcast tool, 174
Whatever (blog), 53
Wikipedia, 159
  on gaming the system, 41
  raising your Klout Score with, 153–155
Will.I.Am, 123
Winfrey, Oprah, 44
Wired magazine, 4
WordPress, 127, 160
Writing, 10, 81

Yelp, 31
YouTube, 95, 194–195
YouTube videos:
  of conferences, 195
  and Klout Score, 171–173
  recommended, 194–195

Zhou, Ding, 6–7, 96, 171
Ziglar, Zig, 10
Zuckerberg, Mark, 144

About the Authors

Gina Carr is a marketing strategist who works with thought leaders and CEOs to leverage social media marketing for more profits, influence, and success. A 20 year serial entrepreneur, Gina has an MBA from the Harvard Business School and engineering degree from the Georgia Institute of Technology. Gina is known around the world as "The Tribe Builder" for her ability to help passionate people build powerful tribes of raving fans for their business or nonprofit organization.

Gina is the dean of the Social Buzz University, www.Social BuzzTraining,com, where she hosts world-class business trainers. She speaks and consults about influence marketing, social scoring, social media, online reputation management, and tribe building. Connect with Gina at www.GinaCarr.com or on Twitter @GinaCarr.

Terry Brock is a globally connected leading authority who works with organizations that want to leverage technology and deploy social media tools for more customer engagement, productivity, and increased profitability. A Hall of Fame Speaker, he regularly delights audiences with entertaining and information-rich presentations that help solve real-world problems based on his 30+ years of experience.

Terry is the former chief enterprise blogger for Skype and former editor-in-chief for AT&T's Networking Exchange blog (over 100 authors). He is a Keynote Speaker known for presenting in a fun, engaging style that delights audiences as they learn practical ways to implement social media principles like Klout with Twitter, Facebook, Linkedin, and other Networks. Connect with Terry at http://www.TerryBrock.com.or through Twitter, @TerryBrock.